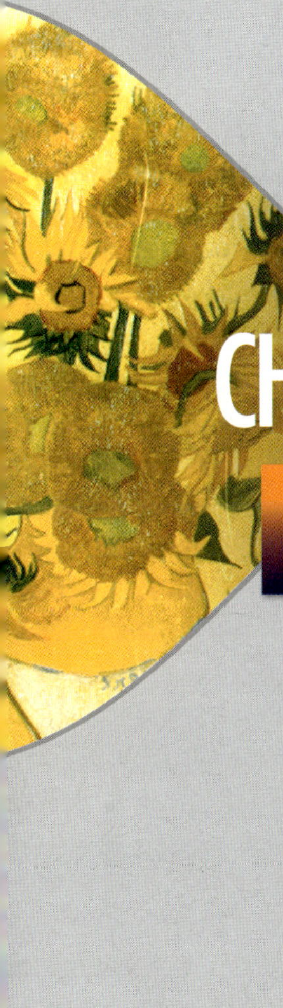

A COMPARISON BETWEEN CHINESE AND WESTERN PAINTINGS

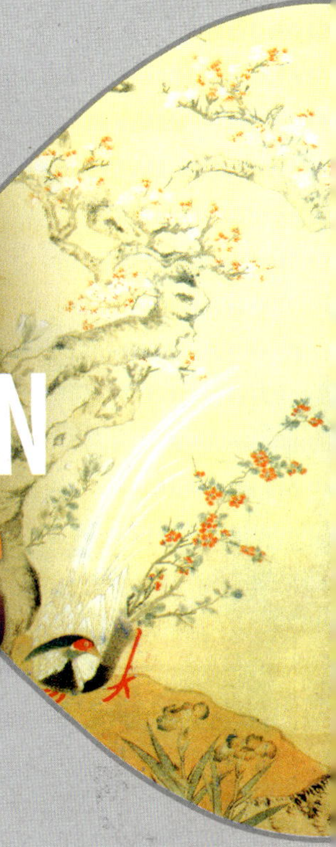

Compiled by
Wu Jing

Printed in China

CHINA INTERCONTINENTAL PRESS

图书在版编目（CIP）数据：

中西绘画比较：英文／吴菁著，王国振等译．—北京：五洲传播出版社， 2008.3

（中西文化比较丛书）

ISBN 978-7-5085-1271-6

Ⅰ．中．．． Ⅱ．①吴．．．②王．．． Ⅲ．绘画－对比研究－中国、西方国家－英文 Ⅳ．J205.1

中国版本图书馆 CIP 数据核字（2008）第 035830 号

中西文化比较丛书：

总顾问：王 晨

总策划：李 冰

总监制：郭长建

出版人：李向平

主 编：吴 伟

中西绘画比较

撰 稿：吴 菁

图片提供：吴 菁等

责任编辑：徐醒生／何 云

翻 译：王国振／汉 佳／李 萍

装帧设计：缪 惟／刘豪亮／林国霞

出版发行：五洲传播出版社

社 址：北京市海淀区莲花池东路北小马厂6号华天大厦

邮政编码：100038

电 话：010-58891281

传 真：010-58891281

制版单位：北京锦绣圣艺文化发展有限公司

印 刷：北京嘉彩印刷有限公司

开 本：787x1092 1/16

印 张：9

印 数：1-5000册

版 次：2008年3月第1版 2008年3月第1次印刷

定 价：79.00元

Contents

Chapter III: Express in a Flat Way and Place Feelings on the Landscape

——A Comparison of the Tendency in Themes between Chinese and Western Paintings

Chapter IV: Colours and Inks

——A Comparison of Colour Concepts and Usage between Chinese and Western Paintings

Chapter V: Rich-colour Painting and Light Water-ink Painting

——Arison of Skills between Chinese and Western Paintings

Chapter VI: Dialectics between Motion and Rest

——Comparison of Representational Forms between Chinese and Western Paintings

Appendix: A Brief Introduction to Chinese and Western Painting Materials

Preface

Both Chinese and Western paintings have a wide range of contents. The book aims to help readers gain an understanding of the Chinese painting and the cultural content that lies behind the Chinese painting. However, limited by the length of writing, the author focuses on the traditional Chinese paintings and European paintings in the 19th century and before.

The fundamental difference between western and traditional Chinese paintings is the one between focus and scattered-points perspective. This author compares the two kinds of paintings in a scattered-points way according to a Chinese scattered-points perspective.

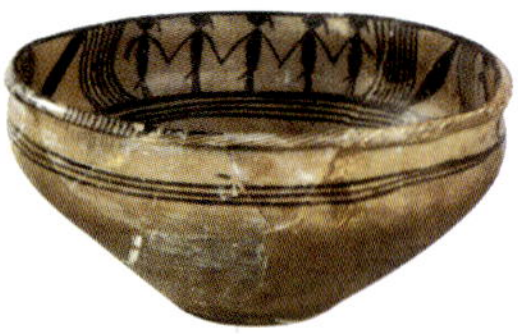

Chapter I : The Expression of Individualities and Psychological Self Comfort

——The Comparison of Historical Roles between Chinese and Western Paintings

Each stage of development in Chinese and western paintings occurred at different times and in a different order. The development of each stage of either one witnessed overlapping phenomena but both of them experienced four stages i.e. rock paintings, paintings on objects such as pottery and handicrafts, religious mural paintings and independent individual paintings. Since he is not introducing the history of painting this author will compare the roles of paintings according to the four stages.

The Carrier for Records of Human Events in Early Times - Rock and Cave Paintings

In 1879 cave paintings were found which were done by people 12,000 to 18,000 years ago during the Palaeolithic Age in Altamira Cave near the northern coast of Spain. In the paintings are images of different animals such as bison, reindeer and horses that are in different poses standing, lying and kneeling down. These animal

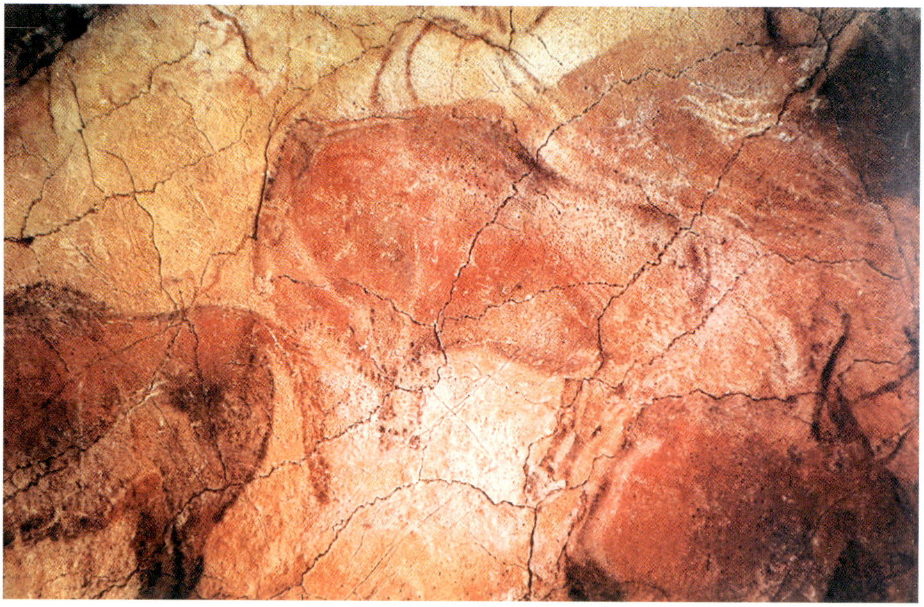

Bison: Old Stone Age cave mural of 185 cm. Discovered in Altamira Cave near the northern coast of Spain.
The bison in the paintings with dimensional shape have dear muscle and skeleton.

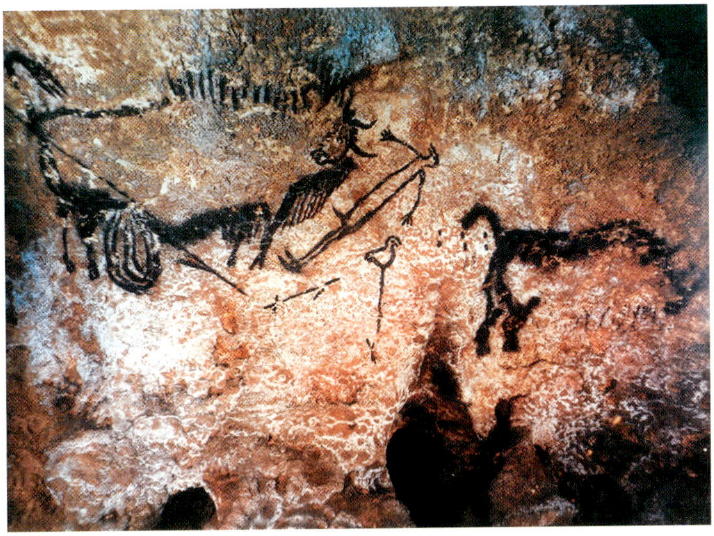

Bison and Wounded Hunter: Old Stone Age cave mural of 185 cm. Discovered in Konak Cave of France.
Murals of this period depict stories.

images not only have clear shapes but they also have clear and precise muscle and skeleton structures and have some basic colour in them. The discovery of these paintings indicates when man's mental development came to a higher stage. Man could see the images in real life and his brain could guide his hands to represent them faithfully on the walls of a cave.

Cave murals from the Palaeolithic Age were also found in France at Lascaux. These depicted animals such as wild goats and a wild ox and a hunter painted in a mixture of coloured minerals and animal blood on the cave wall. The rock painting of a wild ox and a hunter on the wall of Lascaux Cave shows some differences from other early rock paintings. This painting showed actions as well as the animals. For example the head of a wild ox had a spear in it and its bowels appear to be running out but it still kept its life like appearance with its erect mane. Also we can see a man with an animal head lying on the ground with both hands open and a piece of a weapon beside him and before the sharp-pointed horns of a wild animal. The appearance of a plot in the painting indicates people were able to express and narrate

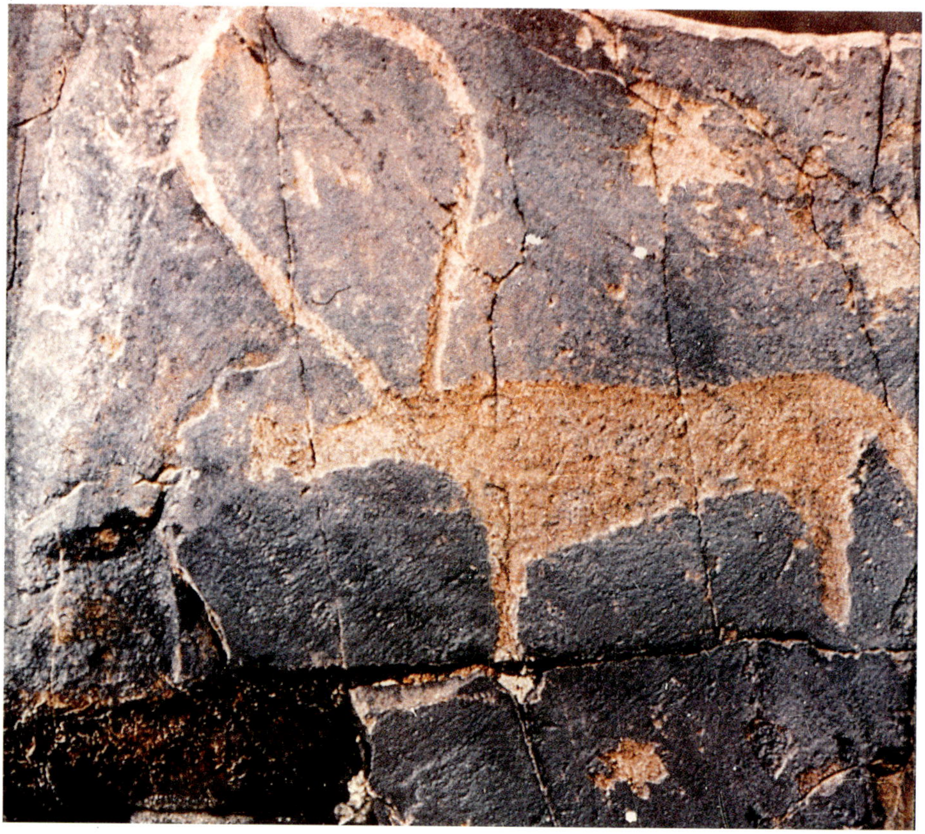

Bison: New Stone Age colored cliff painting found in Altay of Xinjiang.
It features Chinese characteristics, plane silhouette.

things by painting.

On a cliff on the Scandinavian Peninsula are the pictures of moose, fish and men painted by chiselling, carving and colouring around 2,000 BC. The appearance of cliff paintings indicates that people at that time had extended their visual activities to outdoor spaces, implying that man's survival ability gradually became stronger and his orbit began to expand. In terms of methods of painting man's handicraft skills were enhanced and now we can see he could chisel and carve as well as paint.

Ancient rock paintings have also been found in northern, western and southern

China. The appearance of rock paintings in China involves a large time span. Generally speaking, the rock paintings appeared from the Neolithic Age to the Bronze Age (about 50,000 years ago to the 2nd century BC) in northern areas such as Ningxia, Xinjiang and the Northeast and during a period 2,000 to 3,000 years ago in most areas in southern China.

The rock paintings were mostly carved out in the north and painted in the south. In the north there are main kinds of carvings. The first is to grind some hard materials on the painting area and there was no outline in contrast against the picture. The second is to chisel. Some very hard pointed article was used like a chisel to carve out the images on the rock. The third was line carving where a very sharp pointed, hard tool was used to carve out deep outlines of the images. Grinding and chiselling produced pictures by changing the original texture of the rocks. By grinding, the texture of the picture area became smoother and flatter than the original rock surface. By chiselling, the texture of the picture area became rougher than the original rock surface. The rock paintings in the south were mostly painted using fingers or feathers as pens. The colours were made from the mixture of hematite powder and animal blood. Both the carved paintings in the north and the coloured paintings in the south are characterized by rough sketches which looked like characterized outlined shadows of men and animals printed on the cliff.

We can conclude that in early times after the emergence of man, people in China and the West had a similar way of living. Man survived at that time by hunting animals and collecting natural fruits, herbs and plants. The major difference between man and animal at that time is that animals only attacked other weaker animals while man, depending on his relatively higher developed brain, made simple tools and dared to attack animals stronger and fiercer than him. Compared to the other animals in nature man was not far ahead in survival abilities. In the course of fighting against animals man often suffered miserable, severe defeats and sacrificed fellow men sometimes. When he gained victory over animals, especially the large ones, it could bring huge happiness and sense of success to all involved. It is hard for us today to understand such feelings as man was very proud of conquering a large animal then is no less than people today who are proud of travelling in outer space. Such happiness and sense of pride needed to be represented and recorded in some way and rock paintings were ideally suited for this demand. In the view of ancient people, flat stones were an ideal material and the painting of real scenes on stones would never change. Therefore the ancestors of both eastern and western people recorded their hunting scenes on rocks. The rock paintings at that time played a role like the media do today - they make successful deeds well known, spreading happiness and building up man's confidence in his own ability. The birth of rock paintings was the result of both needing to record and to boast about the important events in people's lives.

Pottery Decoration and Decorations on Other Wares

In the course of the development from rock paintings to independent canvas and paper paintings as a means of display both China and the West experienced the transition with other materials as painting mediums.

In the history of both China and the West pottery was used as an important medium of painting. Their ways of painting were completely different mainly because of the different development in their societies.

In the 12th century BC pottery ware and its decoration became a fine art in the ancient Greek civilization. In the 3rd century BC, in the West, pottery painting had changed from geometric designs to representative painting with strong realism. If these paintings were transplanted to a flat even surface they would be realistic paintings.

Pottery decoration in China reached its peak during the Neolithic Age, in Primitive Society before the 21st century BC, when most of the pottery paintings were geometric designs and rough sketches.

Notwithstanding the different ways of painting and period, generally speaking, pottery designs of both the east and west mainly played the role of decoration compared to rock paintings. When pottery painting came into being, almost no animal on earth could threaten the normal life of man. The time had arrived where man could conquer and even domesticate, by his intelligence and skills, those animals that threatened him before. Man had changed from a hunter gatherer to the more stable land husbandry and he could spare time to decorate his life by painting in order to satisfy the spiritual demands for happiness.

Besides pottery, Chinese painting had experienced the transition to various other mediums such as metal, wood, stone and brick from rock paintings and then to silk and paper paintings.

After 2,100 BC, with continuous improvements in intelligence and skills, the ancient Chinese became increasingly active in exploring nature and gradually found different metals and grasped the art of metallurgy. So the eastern man shifted his interest from pottery to metal products and remained highly passionate in his research and development of the craftwork of metals and also lacquer ware from 1,

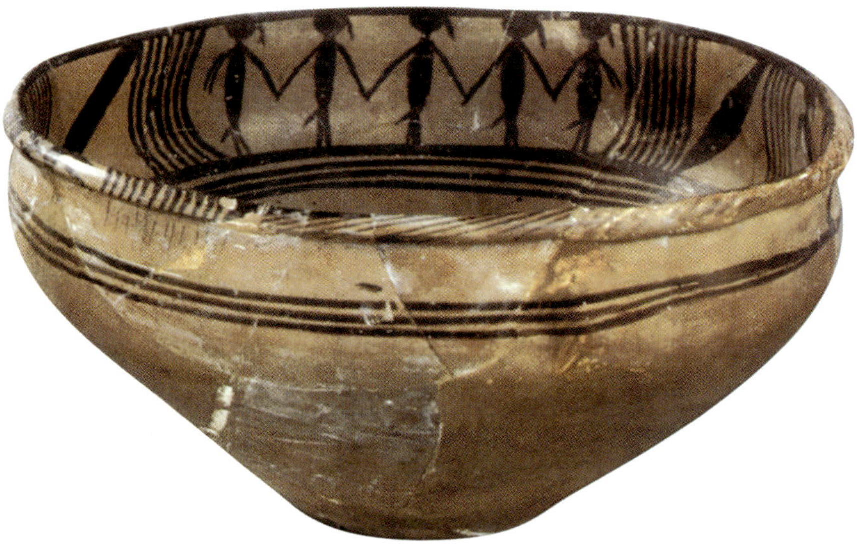

Colored Pottery Basin With Dancing Patterns: New Stone Age pottery of 14.1 cm, discovered from Sunjia Village in Qinghai. Preserved in the China History Museum.

Pottery is also the carries of Chinese paintings.

600 to 221 BC. Pottery did not disappear accordingly but the attention on pottery decoration weakened to a large extent. At that time people paid attention to the improvement of their production technology (researching ceramic glaze) instead of painting and decorating pottery.

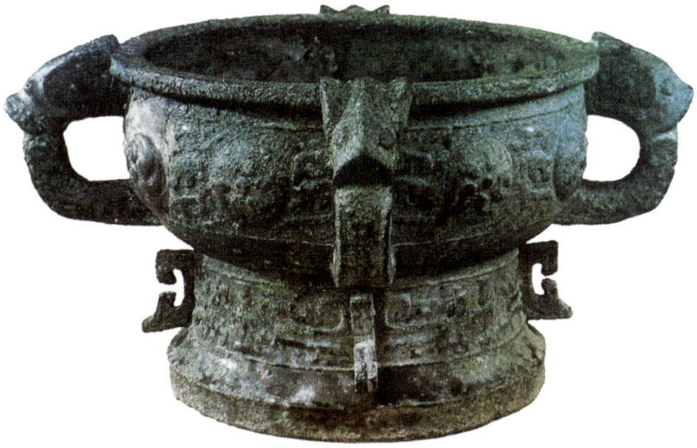

Yihou Shigui Bronze Ware from the Western Zhou Dynasty: Unearthed from Dantu, Jiangsu, it is 15.7 cm high with the diameter of the mouth 22.5 cm. Preserved in the China History Museum.

In the 11th century BC the Zhou Dynasty (1100-221 BC) was established in China and as a result the sovereignty of the Emperor Zhou, a tyrant of the Shang Dynasty (16-11 cent. BC) who extorted excessive taxes was turned over and the society became much more stable than before. This offered a good environment for a substantial increase in production and cultural development. Painting began to break away from craftwork and started an independent branch. From the 8th century BC to 221 BC China entered the Spring and Autumn Period (770-476 BC) and suffered again the chaos caused by war with several independent regimes set up by force of arms. Fortunately each comparatively independent prince's regime witnessed a high production activity. On the one hand they dealt actively with border warfare and on the other hand they developed their culture and enjoyed their lives in the free and peaceful climate removed from war. From 1600 to 221 BC, the development level of Chinese painting is shown by metalwork and lacquer decorations and also unearthed silk paintings.

Yihou Shigui, a piece of bronze ware from the Western Zhou Dynasty (1046 - 771 BC), was unearthed from Dantu, Jiangsu. It is 15.7 cm high with the diameter of the mouth 22.5 cm. In ancient times it was used as a vessel for holding food. The body was decorated with whirl lines and designs of transfigured Kui (a one-legged monster in Chinese fable) dragons. The dragon design became indispensable in the decoration of all the past dynasties in China. It was the symbol of both China and the supreme authority in China.

On a silver mirror inlaid with gold produced during the Warring States Period (475-221 BC) a scene was painted of a warrior with a sword in his hand intending to kill a tiger. At that time the situation was tense with fierce battles on the frontline while at the rear people led peaceful and relaxed lives and this influenced art greatly. Motion and rest were now combined in art. This piece of work is a typical representation of that time. The war horse was startled and bug-eyed and had its mouth slightly open and its hoof and tail raised. Its fear of the

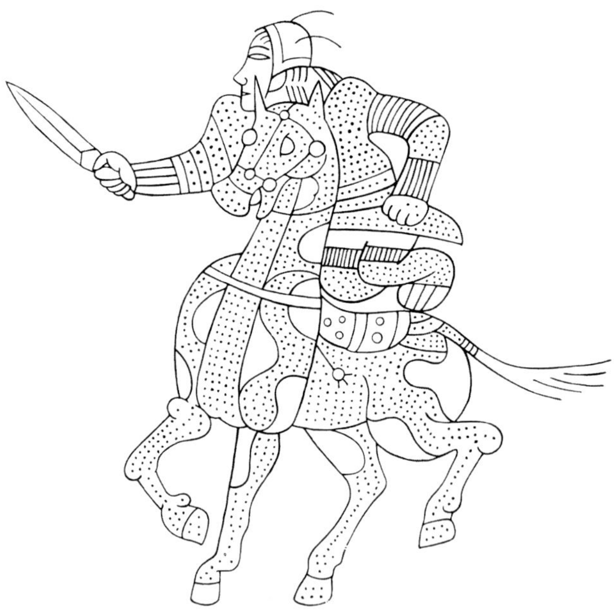

Silver Mirror Inlaid With Gold and Painted of a Warrior With a Sword in His Hand Intending to Kill a Tiger: Warring States Period (475-221 BC). Unearthed from Jincun Ancient Tomb in Luoyang.

tiger sets off the warrior's steadiness and bravery. The curve from the back of the tiger's neck to its tail is fluent and strong showing tensile force and intensifying its cohesion. The confrontation of the two composes the sense of force and tension by the strong contrast between motion and rest. Chinese painting during the Warring States Period (475-221 BC) was characterized by the tendency in using extended and forceful curves. The decorations on "Yanle (conviviality) Gongzhan (battle) Pot" (a piece of bronze ware produced in the Warring States Period (475-221 BC)) are mostly such lines to compose the outlines of figures and animals. Meanwhile the decorative designs represented life at that time, going to battle while developing production at the same time.

After the pottery decoration era Chinese painting did not shift to metal ware but continued to develop using such mediums as lacquer ware, stone tablets and building bricks. It is not hard to understand the reason for this progression: people used slender pointed pieces of bamboo or other soft tools like pens to paint decorations on pottery surfaces, while the metal wares were mainly cast in a foundry and were not suitable for painting. As to stone and brick carving, a pen could be replaced by a knife to etch decorations and as to lacquer ware, the method and tools were similar to those for pottery. Silk was also used as a painting surface at the same time as lacquer ware, building stone slates and building bricks. Silk has a very smooth surface and any writing on it is not constrained, so it is very suitable for painting and writing. Therefore it was necessary for painting to develop independently from pottery decoration.

According to the records in *Shi Ji (Historical Records)*, independent painting had emerged during the Shang Dynasty (1600 - 1046 BC) and woven products and buildings were painted with decorations. Till the Spring and Autumn Period (770-

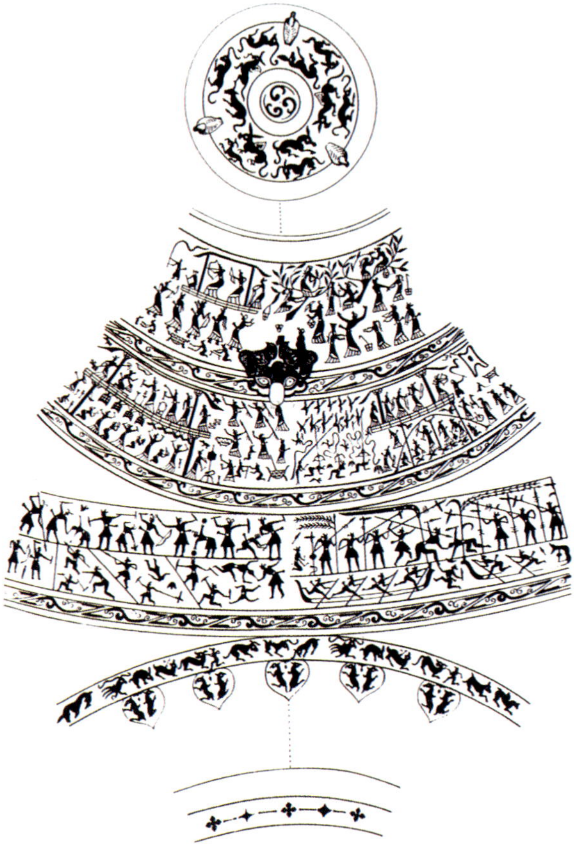

Rubbings of "*Yanle (Conviviality) Gongzhan (Battle) Pot*", a piece of bronze ware produced in the Warring States Period (475-221 BC)

476 BC), painting had a wider range of use. It is said that the independent paintings at that time aimed at illustrating moral education. Until today no extant works of murals, woven-product paintings or independent paintings before the Spring and Autumn Period (770-476 BC) have been found. The silk paintings of figures like the Dragon and Phoenix and the Imperial Dragon from the Warring States Period (475-221 BC) are the oldest extant independent paintings in China and the style is definitely from the Warring States period. The most important character of the Warring States Period painting is its superiority over shadow - like portraits and the depiction of specific and subtle places by lines.

There are many paintings from the period of the Qin and Han dynasties from 221 BC to the 3rd century AD but they are mostly represented by a combination with craftwork, such as the figure bricks of the Qin Dynasty (221 - 206 BC) and the figure stone tablets, the eaves tiles (building components with picture decorations), silk paintings, lacquer paintings, wood-block paintings and mural paintings. According to literature records several different classes of painters had appeared during the Han Dynasty such as the imperial, the literati and the folk painters. According to *The Records of Famous Paintings of Past Dynasties* by Zhang Yanyuan, Zhang Heng (78-139), a scientist of the Eastern Han Dynasty (24-220 AD), and Cai Yong (132-192), a musician of the Eastern Han Dynasty, were both literati painters of that time. Unfortunately none of their paintings still exist. The Silk Road was opened during the reign of the Emperor Wudi (157-87 BC) of the Han Dynasty which strengthened Chinese communications in economy and culture with the countries in Western Asia. China's economic power gradually became stronger and it became a power then. Therefore the painting of the Han Dynasty not only inherited the vigorous style from before but also added a natural and graceful style.

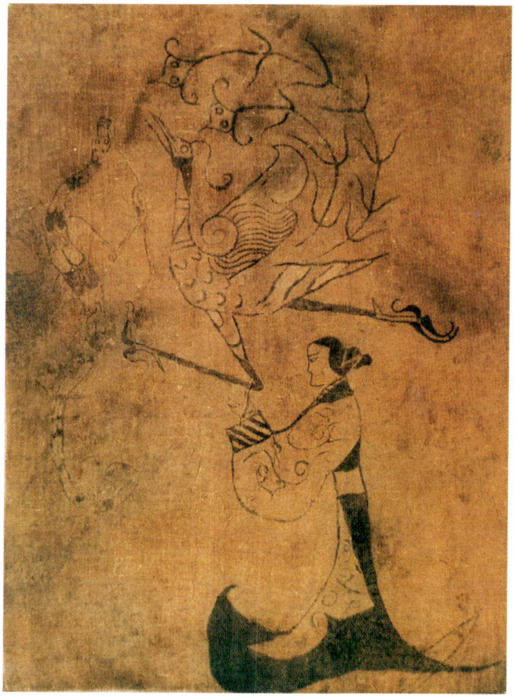

Silk Paintings of Dragon and Phoenix: Warring States Period (475 BC-221 BC). Unearthed from Chengjia Dashan, Changsha, Hunan Province, the silk painting, measuring 31.2x23.2 cm, it is preserved in the Hunan Museum.

Its special feature is its superiority over shadow--like portraits and the depiction of specific and subtle places by lines.

It can be concluded that rock painting is a tool used by man to record and prove his survival ability while the decorations on pottery, porcelain and other craftwork was mainly aesthetic while showing man's substantial development and his spiritual innovations. In the course of the development from rock paintings to independent canvas and paper paintings as a means of display both China and thc West experienced the transition with other materials as painting mediums.

PAINTINGS WITH RELIGIOUS THEMES

The growth of man's desire accelerated the progress in technology and enriched materials. Vice versa, the development in substance accelerated the growth of man's desire. Some people became envious of and desired to occupy others' innovations and they took action, plundering before destroying. In history many cultures were destroyed in this way, for example, the ancient Roman Culture and the Egyptian Civilization were plundered and destroyed and the Eight-power Allied Forces that came and looted China. Man suffered severe misery and pain between creation and destruction and between invasion and occupation. Man's soul demanded a comfort and a supreme authority for maintaining normal living order and that is how religion came into being. After the emergence of religion man became conscious and willing to help propagate religious doctrines and painting was one of the ways.

In the 4th century AD the Huns occupied Chang'an (Xi'an of Shaanxi today) and turned over the Western Jin Dynasty (265-316). They then pushed forward to Rome and seriously damaged the Rome Empire. Along with looting by other forces simultaneously the Roman Empire collapsed.

In the west, Christianity, which had always been an underground religion, was recognized as a legitimate religion by the Roman government in the early 4th

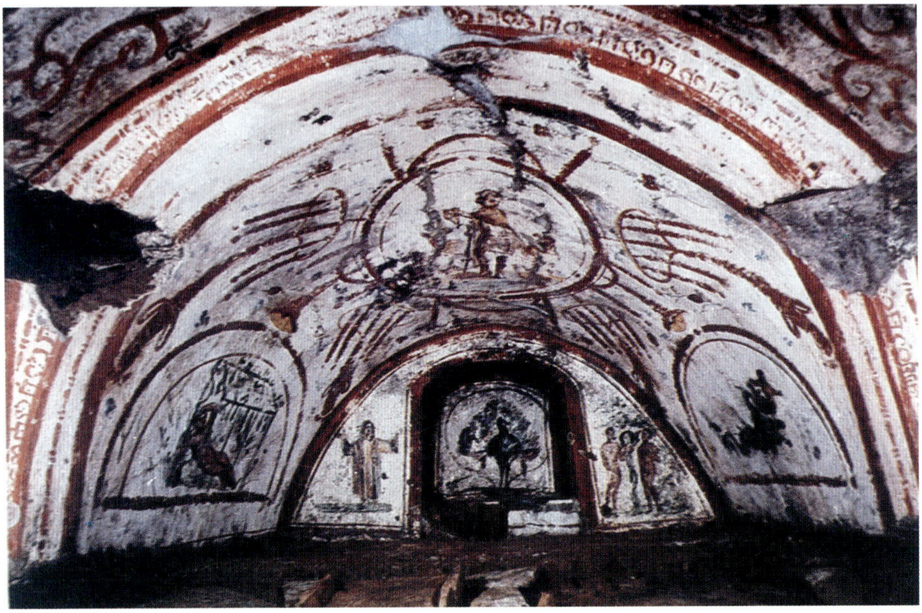

Tomb Chamber and Murals: Middle and later period of the 4th century. Rome

Christianity spread secretly in Rome in the 1st and 2nd centuries. When Christians died they were buried in a same cave tomb,and the cave also became the gathering place for Christians. Symbols of Bible were painted on the tomb walls. This was the source of Christian paintings.

century. Then relevant religious murals and paintings with religious themes emerged at this historical moment and became the leading theme of medieval paintings. This also established an important basis for the prosperity of European oil paintings later. The mural paintings and stone carvings of inner and outer coffins related to Christianity in former graves were represented before people. In order to enlarge and spread Christian doctrines, hand - written and painted copies of Christian ideals became popular in the west in the 4th century AD. From the 8th to 10th century Bible, Gospel and calendar books related to farming became very popular. At that time as to the painting of books, importance was attached to the cover, illustration and decoration of initials. The Bible and the Gospel pay attention to man’s soul and the farming calendar is related to man's fundamental living, which means people of that time equated spiritual purification to the importance of survival. During this period paintings preferred to play the role of propaganda.

The prevalence of Buddhism also changed the role and style of Chinese painting. From 220 to 589 AD, China was in chaos caused by wars with independent regimes during the Three Kingdoms (220-280 AD), Western and Eastern Jin (265-420 AD), and Northern and Southern Dynasties (386-589 AD). The unstable living conditions caused by war could not be changed by common individuals. Due to their dissatisfaction with real life people put their hopes in religion. The Buddhism that was introduced into China around the 1st century AD became popular around the 4th century AD. People began to build large Buddhist grottoes and relevant sculptures and murals also developed. This caused the original murals of the 2nd and 3rd centuries to be considered mature. War, in addition to causing religion to become popular also accelerated cultural exchanges and combinations between the different nationalities. Religious murals were also helpful in cultural exchanges. The Kizil Grottoes and Dunhuang Grottoes show distinctive traces of cultural exchanges between different nationalities. The clarity and exaggeration of motion in figure structures on the mural paintings in the Kizil Grottoes came evidently from Indian culture. The use of bright colours like red and green and the style of dress and adornments were definitely drawn from the local region of Xinjiang and the tendency of lines clearly shows the style of the Han Dynasty (206 BC - 220 AD).

During the Wei, Jin and Northern and Southern dynasties (220-589 AD), the most successful painters recorded in historical books include Cao Buxing, Wei Xie, Dai Kui, Gu Kaizhi, Lu Tanwei, Zhang Sengyao, Jiang Shaoyou, Yang Zihua and Cao Zhongda. Most of them were from southern China but drew on the vigour in northern stone carvings for inspiration. Their painting lines show some toughness.

It should be said that the period of the Wei, Jin and Northern and Southern dynasties (220-589 AD) is an important time for the development of Chinese painting. If Chinese painting is compared to a large tree the Chinese humanistic folk customs are the soil from which the tree grew. The relevant factors and arts before the time are the unbroken and interlaced roots of the tree and the paintings and religious murals of the time are the joining of the roots and the initial stage of its trunk. The use of lines in Chinese paintings became totally mature during this time.

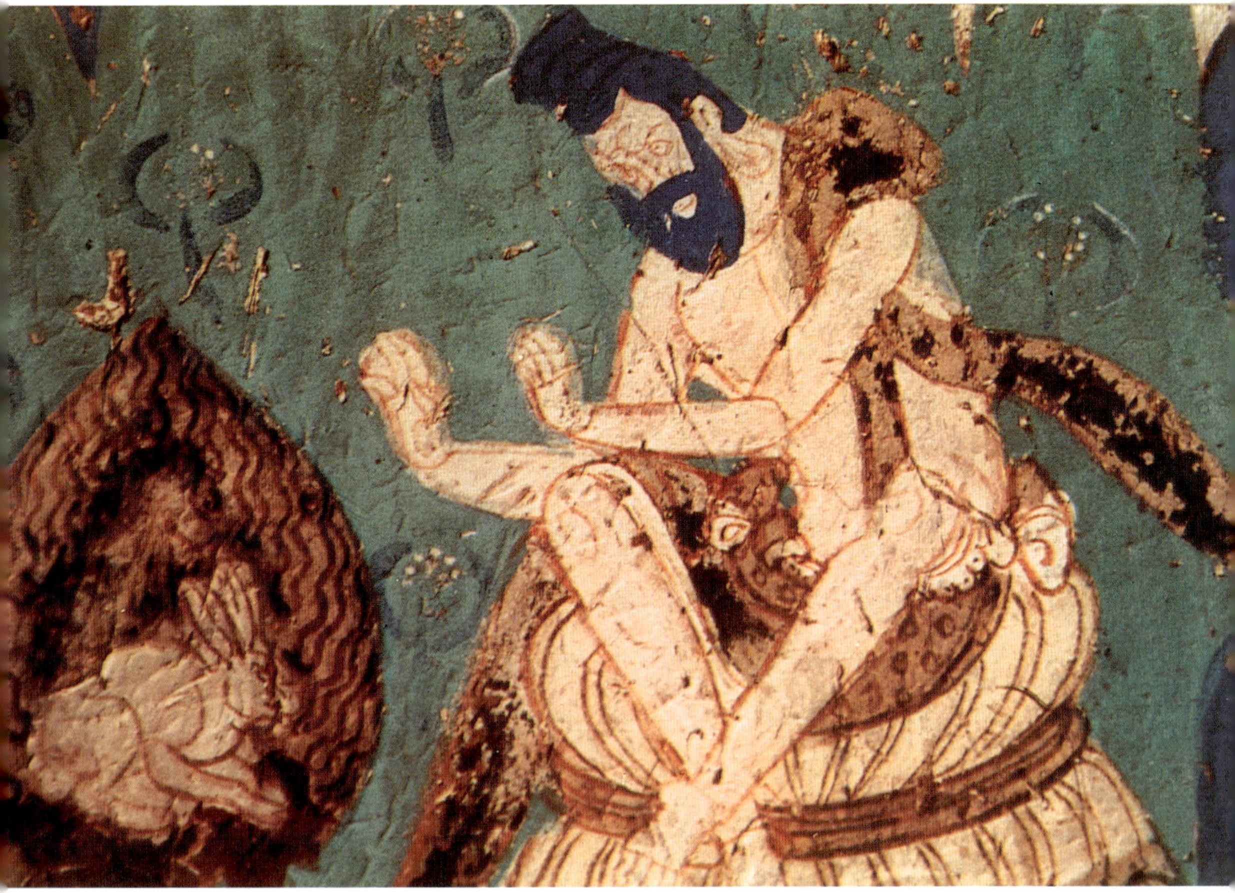

Tuwang Bensheng: Kizil Thousand-Buddha Grottos in Xinjiang, China.

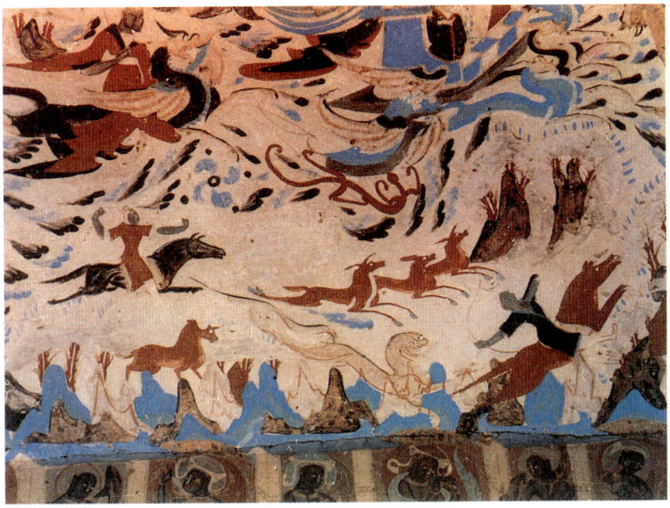

Buddhist fables and parables (Part): Northern Wei Dynasty, Dunhuang No.254 Cave, Fresco, 165 x172cm

This founded the base for later Chinese paintings with lines as a means of representation. The bright colouring and the concave - convex demitint in religious murals made full preparation for realistic painting with bright colours. The echo between religion and idle talk in metaphysics was in tune with the high-hearted literati indulging in self-admiration. This later urged paintings to break away from propaganda and shift to the role of placing and expressing spirit and ideals and accelerated landscape paintings to develop and prosper for a thousand years after the Tang Dynasty (618-907 AD).

In China around the 4th century AD one of the important roles played by painting was to propagate Buddhism and encourage people to do good deeds. Gu Kaizhi, a painter of the Eastern Jin Dynasty (317-420 AD), produced a famous painting entitled a Picture of Nu Shi Zhen (An Admonition of Female Officials). It is said the painting was done following the Nu Shi Zhen (An Admonition of Female Officials) written by Zhang Hua. At that time China was ruled by the Emperor Huidi of the Jin Dynasty (265-420 AD). The Emperor Huidi was mentally-retarded so his wife Jia Nanfeng controlled the country. She was a narrow-minded and selfish woman and did many merciless things against the stable development of the country. Then

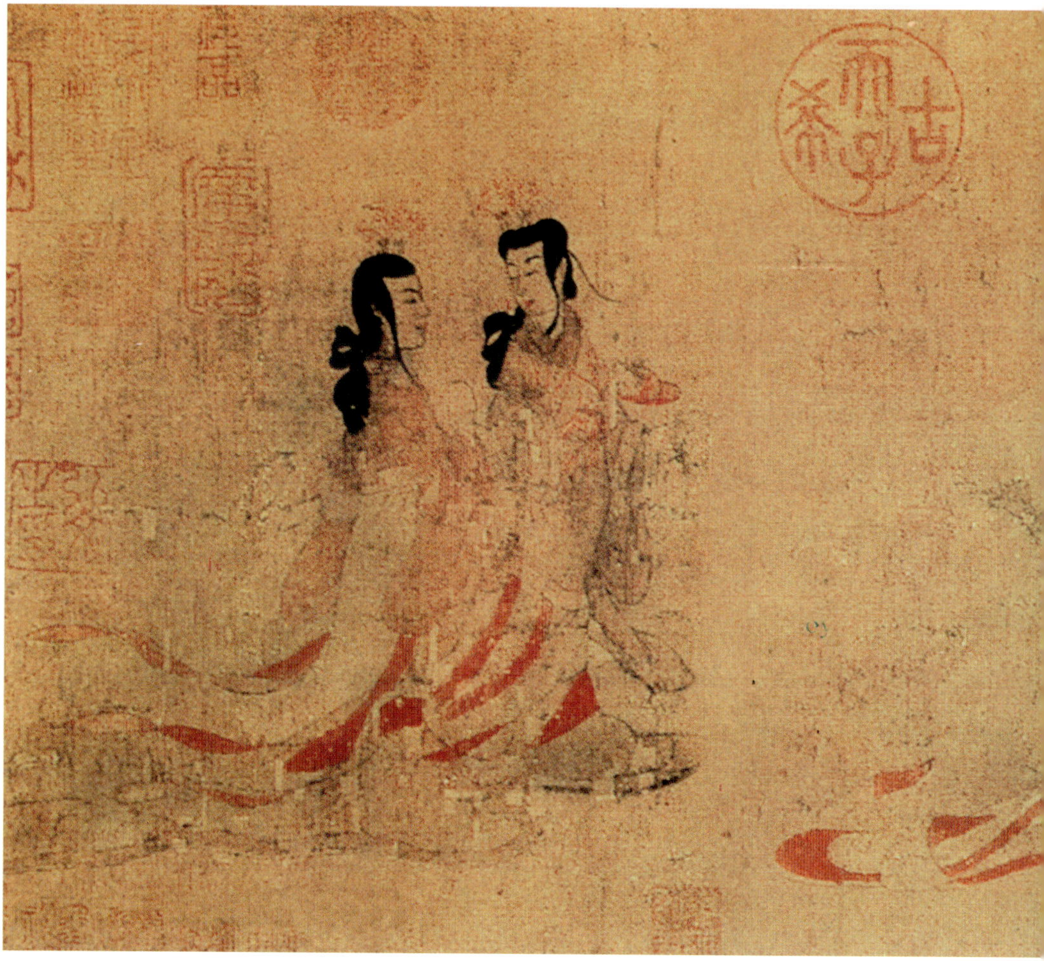

Picture of Nu Shi Zhen (An Admonition of Female Officials) (Part): by Gu Kaizhi in the Eastern Jin Dynasty. Preserved in the British Museum.
Paintings of this period preach in a sense.

Zhang Hua wrote a piece entitled Nu Shi Zhen in which he portrayed the different virtues of 12 female officials so as to admonish politely Jia Nanfeng to retrain herself and do better things. The Picture of Nu Shi Zhen by Gu Kaizhi and Nu Shi Zhen by Zhang Hua both encouraged people to do good deeds.

It is evident that in the 4th century AD both Chinese and western paintings took

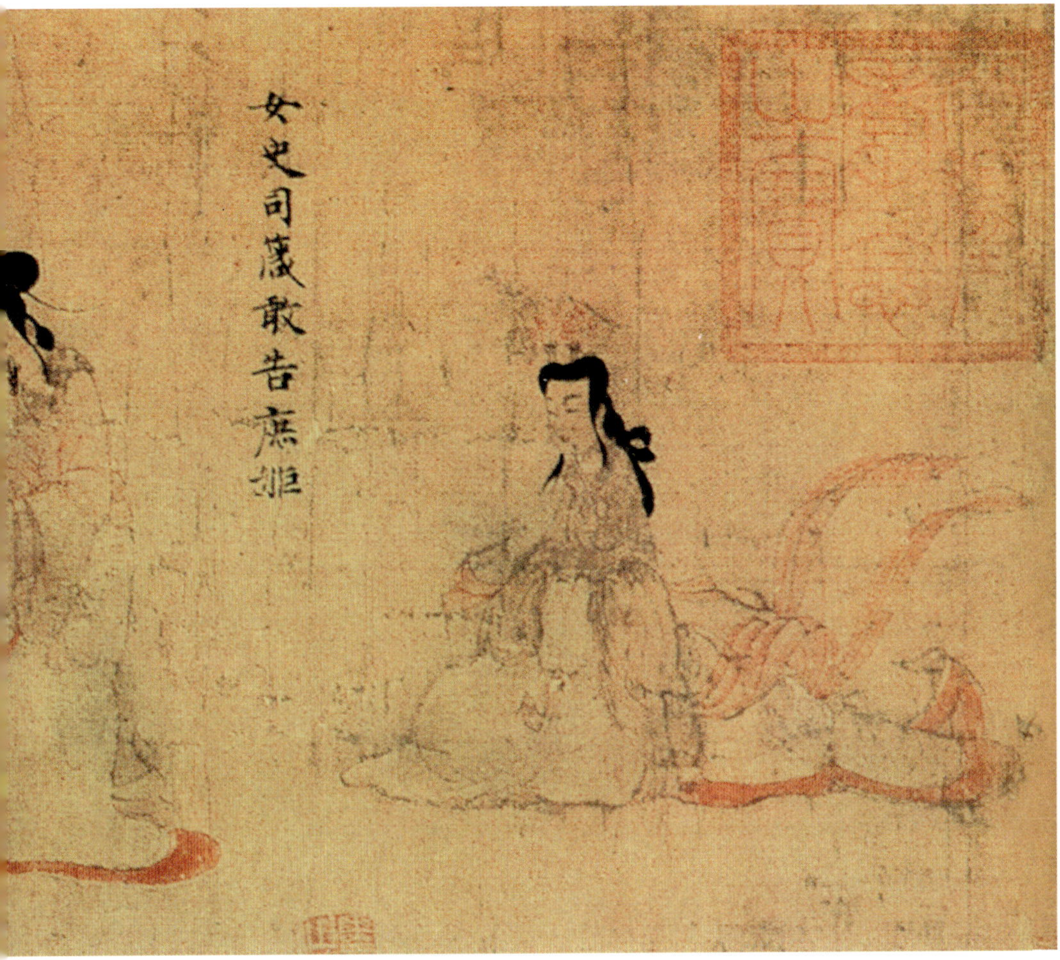

on the responsibility of morals as well as decoration.

Religious mural painting is a watershed. After the 4th century AD and especially after the 10th century big differences appeared between Chinese and western paintings.

WESTERN PAINTINGS FROM THE ALTAR TO A MAN'S WORLD

After the 10th century the West entered the Middle Ages. Western paintings mainly shouldered the role of propaganda until the 18th century. The Renaissance in the 15th century is a turning point for western paintings. A philosopher once said that progress in the West evolved around the struggle between science and religion and when science advanced one step religion withdrew one step. The Renaissance corroborated such a theory. After following religion blindly for a long time and with the continuous improvement of science, man's confidence was enhanced further. He possessed a stronger independent consciousness, his ego woke up in his heart and he acknowledged caring about himself and then he put forward ideas about humanism and humanity. People seemed to prefer science in the argument between science and religion. The awakening of their egos made people more aware so they did not blindly follow religion but they became more rational in their belief and abided by their doctrines more realistically. Paintings possessed a new style and look, even those with Biblical themes. Looking at the new paintings, people's consciousness of ego and equality were awakened. From the paintings of the time it can be seen that people shifted their focus of attention from religion to science, man himself and the environment related to man. Although direct depiction of science cannot be seen in the paintings the use of the optical concept of "focus

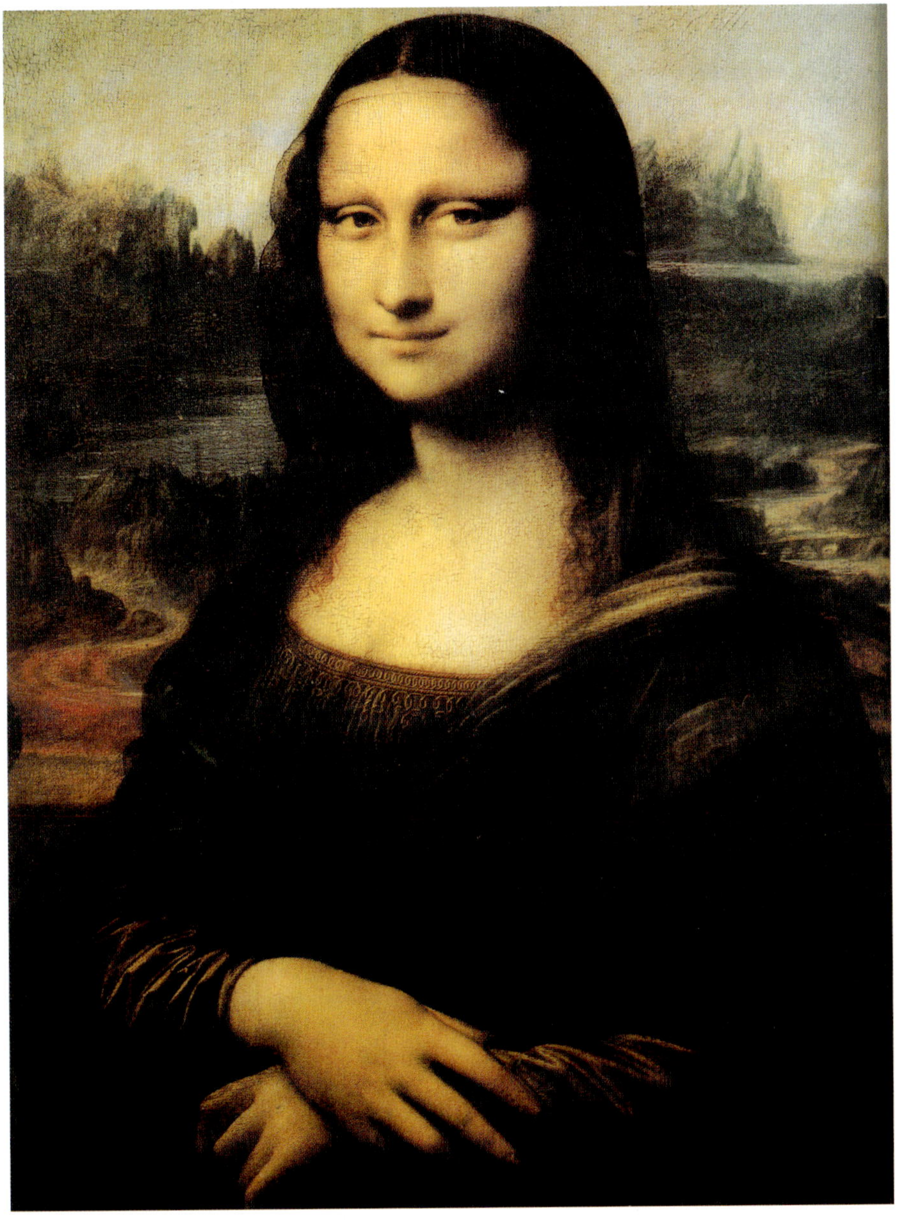

Mona Lisa, 1503-1506, oil painting 77x53 cm, by Leonardo da Vinci of Italy, preserved in the Museum of Louvre in Paris.

Painters of the time liked to place figures either in indoor or outdoor spaces with this perspective. Leonardo da Vinci is one of the best representatives of this style and his masterpieces, The Mona Lisa is a fine examples of its application.

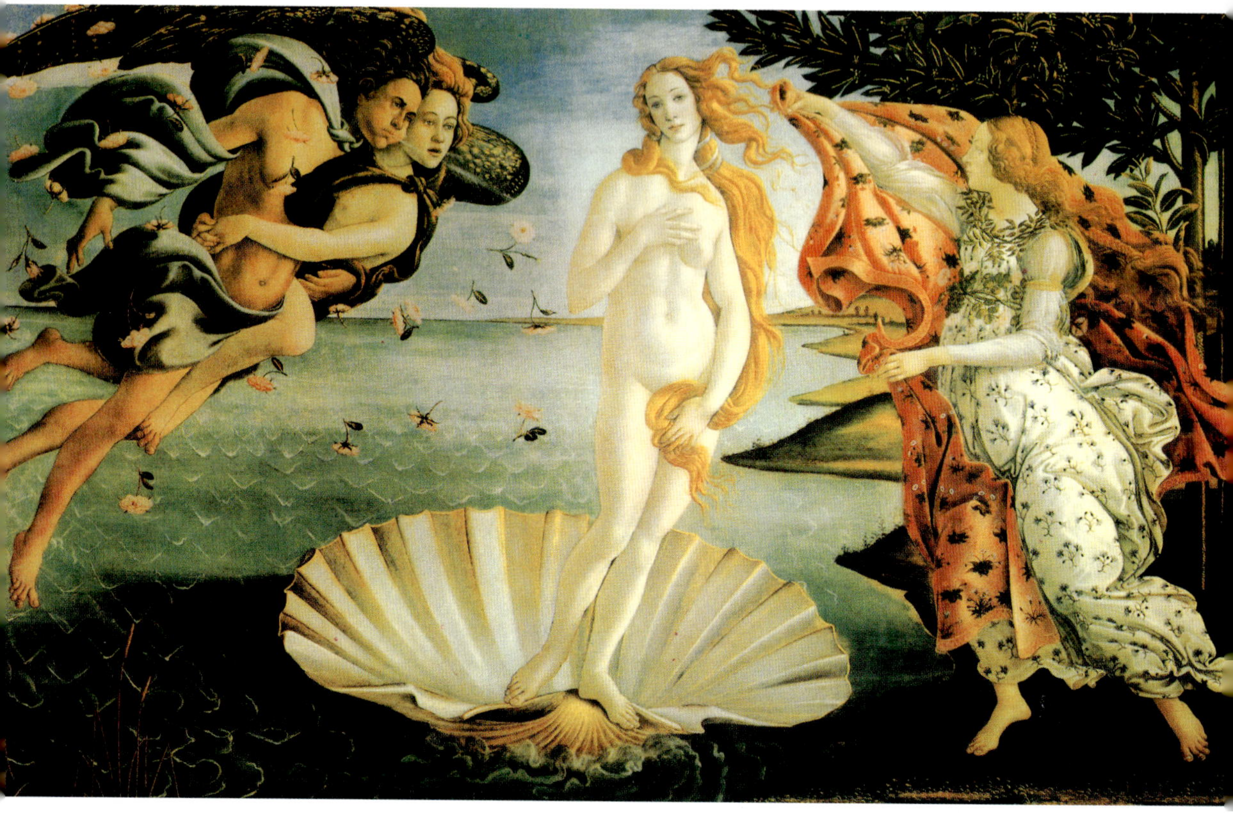

The Birth of Venus: by Sandro Botticelli of Italy, circa 1485, Tempera on canvas 172.5 × 278.5cm, Preserved in the Uffizi Gallery, Florence.

It depicts the goddess Venus, having emerged from the sea as a full grown woman, arriving at the sea-shore. Botticelli used some deformation elements. In those times, it is a bold and creative move. Venus's distressed and confused expression is a beauty that the painter painstakingly seeks. Such expression of the female figures is showed in his most works. It is almost a sign of Botticelli's works.

perspective" is obvious. People became very skilled at using this realistic skill and turned to the exploration of outdoor spaces. Painters of the time liked to place figures either in indoor or outdoor spaces with this perspective. Leonardo da Vinci is one of the best representatives of this style and his masterpieces, *The Last Supper* and *Mona Lisa*, are fine examples of its application.

People did not settle for the representation of a vivid appearance any longer.

In comparison with the time before the Renaissance they attached more importance to the expression of the figures. The smiles of the figures in paintings had less holiness and seriousness but more of the kindness of a man's world and intelligence showed though the eyes of the subjects. At the start of the Renaissance many famous painters emerged with distinct personalities such as Sandro Botticelli (Italian, 1444-1504), Leonardo da Vinci (Italian, 1452-1519), Michelangelo (Italian, 1475-1564), Raphael (Italian, 1483-1520), Titian (Italian, 1477-1576) and Albrecht Durer (German, 1471-1528), to name but a few.

In the 17th century a great painter Rembrandt (1606-1669) appeared in the Netherlands. On the basis of looking for realistic painting he paid more attention to the creation of an atmosphere in a particular situation. In his *Night Watch*, an unprecedented lively and vibrant atmosphere in life was created by the motion and expression of each figure and the treatment of light. His *Man in a Golden Helmet* attracts audiences to enter the painting and sit quietly along with the figure. Rembrandt is only one of the outstanding representatives of European painters in the 17th century. Other famous painters include Peter Paul Rubens (Holland, 1577-

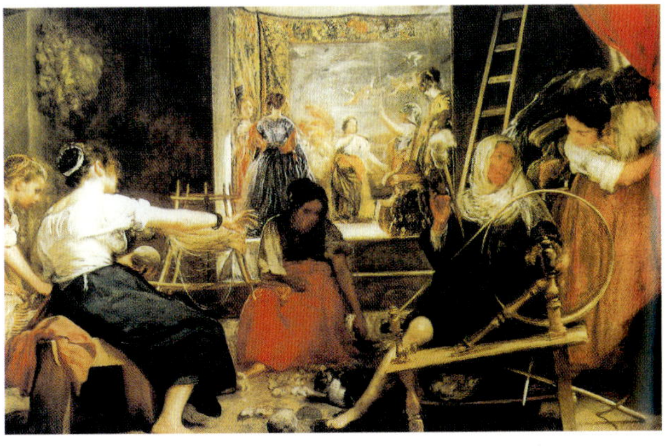

The Spinners: 1657, Oil on Canvas 220 x 293cm, by Diego Velazquez of Spain, Preserved in the Museo del Prado, Madrid.

One of his final works was Las hilanderas (The Spinners), representing the interior of the royal tapestry works. It is full of light, air and movement, featuring vibrant colors and careful handling. Common people appeared in portraits and figure paintings, so that European painting in the 17th century became much more mundane with more emphasis on lifestyle.

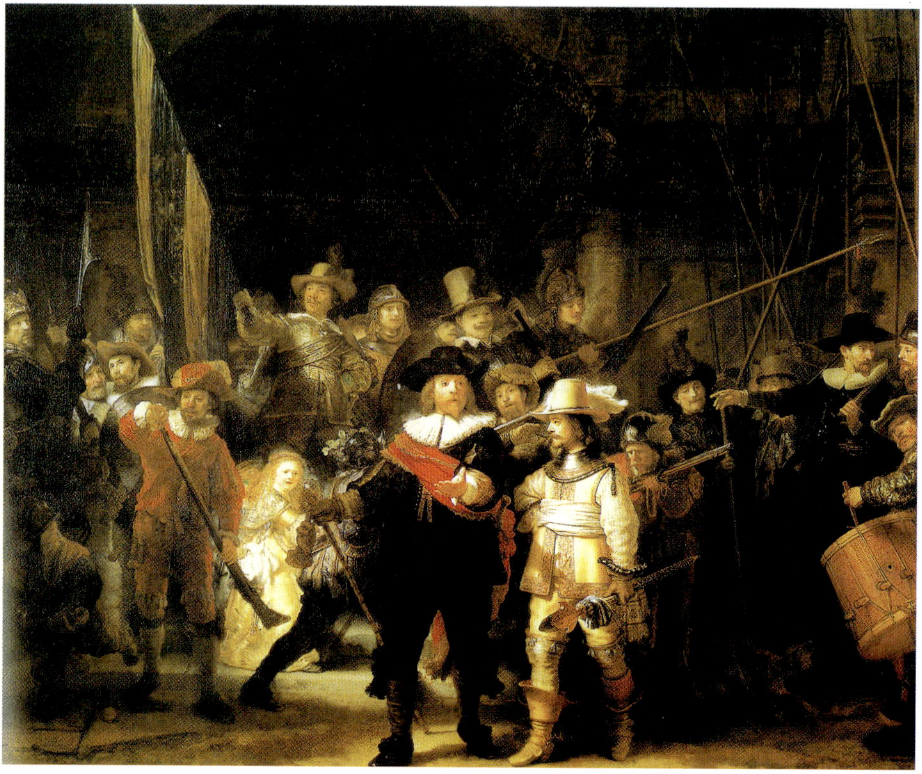

Night Watch: 1642, oil on canvas 363 x 437cm, by Rembrandt of the Netherlands, Preserved in the Amsterdam's Rijksmuseum.

In the Night Watch, an unprecedented lively and vibrant atmosphere in life was created by the motion and expression of each figure and the treatment of light.

1640) and Diego Velazquez (Spanish, 1599-1660).

Generally speaking, European painting in the 17th century became much more mundane with more emphasis on lifestyle. From this time on western painting witnessed significant changes in its subjects and branches. Figures of not only nobles but also common people appeared in portraits and figure paintings such as *The Gypsy Woman* by Hales, and *The Spinners* by Diego Velazquez. Pure landscape paintings appeared without any figures at all such as *View of Delft* by Jan Vermeer, and *The Water Mill* and *The Avenue at Middelharnis* by Hobbema. Thus the independent branch of landscape painting came into being. Still life paintings appeared, such as *Still Life* by Heda, giving rise to the independent branch of still life painting. There also appeared paintings describing circumstances in life, such as the *Love Letter* by Jan Vermeer and *The Sick Woman and a Doctor* by Jan Steen. These paintings appeared because painting was no longer monopolized by churches or governments and middle class and ordinary people began to purchase paintings from painters to decorate their houses. In order to make paintings more suitable for household decoration painters introduced an interesting aspect. They introduced the normal living environment along with daily articles and food common in

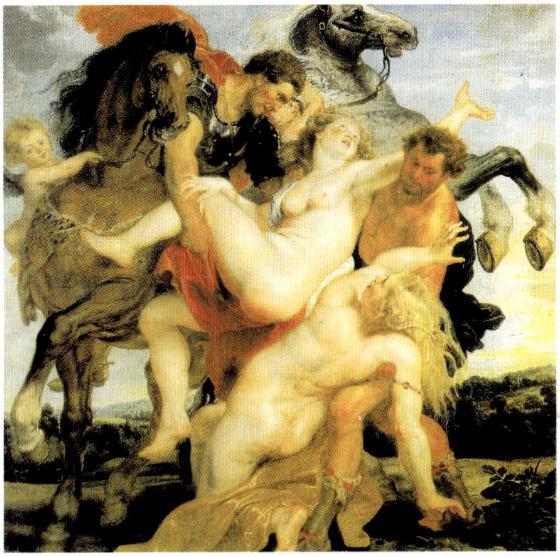

Caster and Pollux Abduct the Daughter of Leukyppos: by Peter Paul Rubens of Flemish, 1615-1617, Oil on Canvas 223 x 209cm, Preserved in the Alte Pinakothek, Munich.

The beautiful and plump body was very worldly and this established a foundation for human body painting at a later time

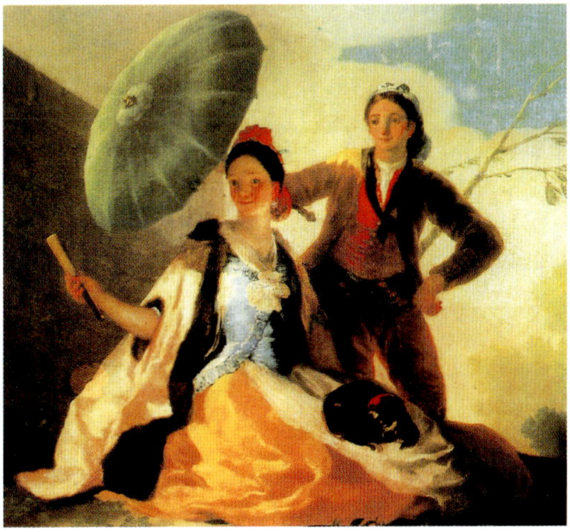

The Sunshade: By Goya of Spain, 1777, oil on canvas 104 x 152cm, Preserved in the Museo del Prado, Madrid.

Goya's imagination is like sunny, brilliant sky without any shade, suspicion and pain. He paid a tribute to the joyance of birth and the beautiful life.

life into their paintings. This was in addition to religious and mythical themes and significant historical events.

After the 17th century western painting witnessed another change. The plots disappeared in figure paintings and the human body became the theme. In the past the human body was more often painted with a plot. Such change implies people's love for life. The most representative painter if this school is Peter Paul Rubens. In many of his works human bodies were still mixed with plots, such as *Caster and Pollus Abduct the Daughter of Leukyppos*, but the beautiful and plump body was very worldly and this established a foundation for human body painting at a later

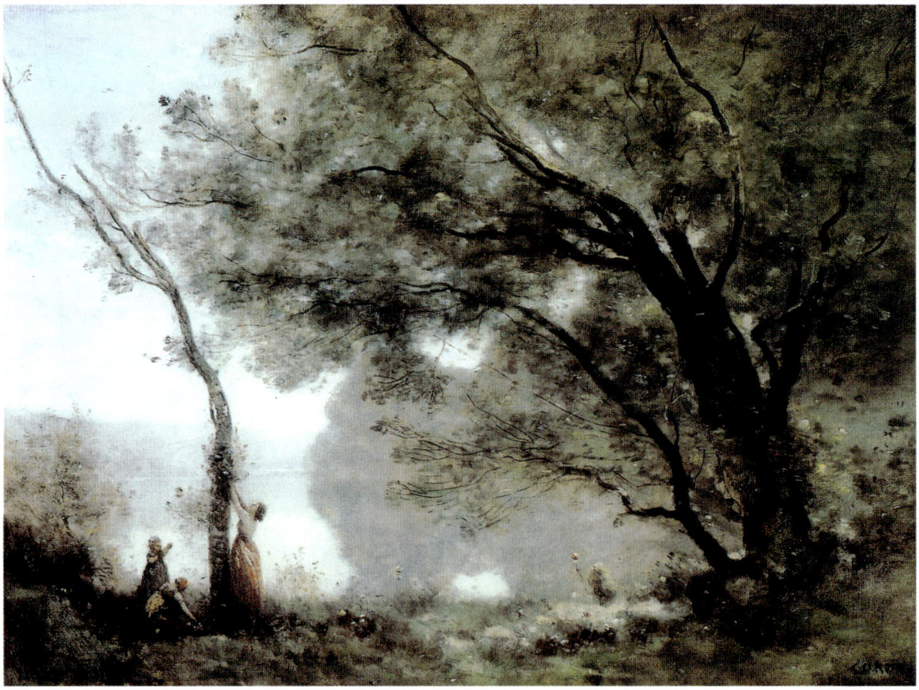

Souvenir de Mortefontaine: by Jean-Baptiste-Camille Corot of France, 1864, oil on canvas 64 x 88cm, Preserved in the Louvre, Paris.

Souvenir de Mortefontaine is Corot's final maturest works as well as one of his landscape masterpieces Compared to the Impressionists who came later, Corot's palette is restrained, dominated with browns and blacks ("forbidden colors" among the Impressionists) along with dark and silvery green.

time.

The painting circle in Europe was more colourful from the 18th and 19th centuries. Goya (a Spanish, 1746-1828), following after Diego Velazquez and David was a painter who cared about current affairs and used them as his creative themes. He painted a batch of satirical cartoon-like etchings focusing on the shortcomings of current politics. After France's invasion of Spain in 1808, Goya did not express his attitude indirectly any longer, but expressed directly his patriotic feelings with paintings such as *The Third of May 1808: The Execution of the Defenders of Madrid* and serial etchings of *The Disasters of War*, etc.

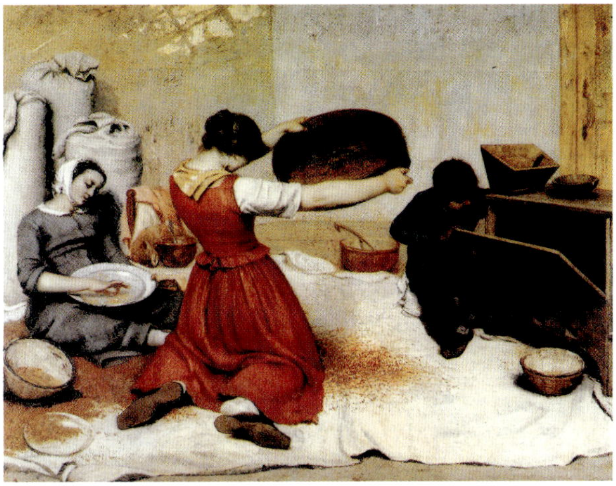

The Wheat Sifters: 1854, oil on canvas 131 x 167cm, by Gustave Courbet of France, preserved in the Nantes Fine Arts Museum. This painting is the expression of Courbet's Realism.

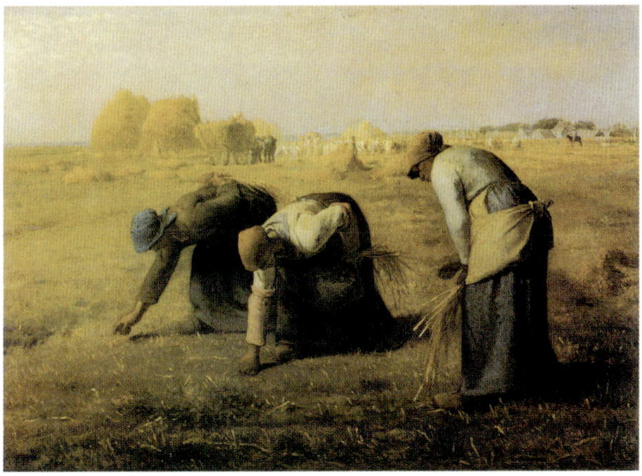

The Gleaners: 1857, oil on canvas, Jean-Francois Millet of France, preserved in the Louvre, Paris.

It depicts three peasant women gleaning a field of stray grains of wheat after the harvest. The painting is famous for monumentalizing what were then the lowest ranks of rural society. The painting was received poorly by the French upper class.

Besides Goya, other painters from the 18th and 19th centuries formed different

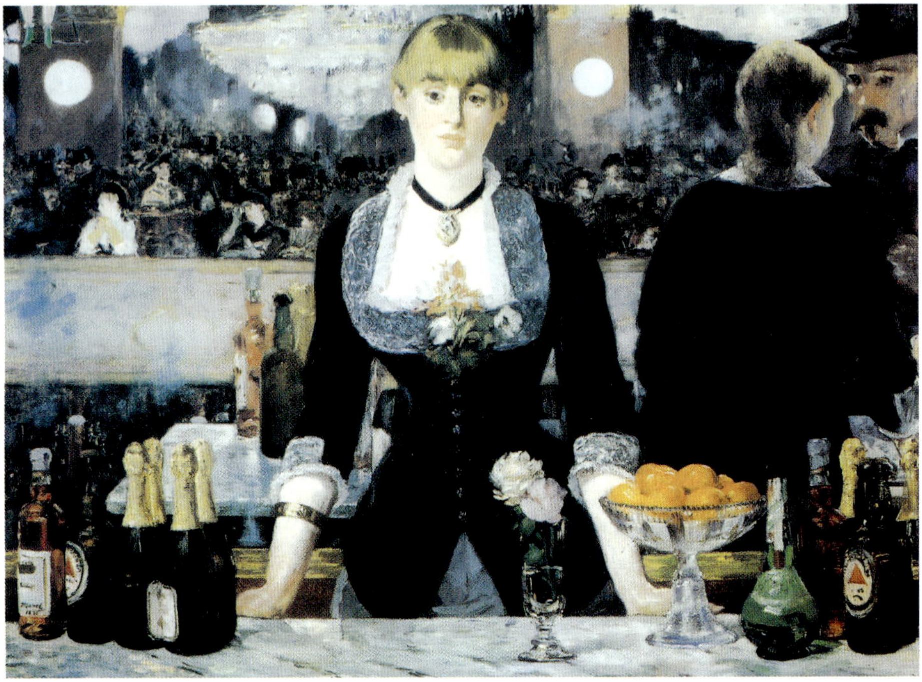

*A Bar at the Folies-Bergere:*1881-1882, oil on canvas, Edouard Manet of France, preserved in the Courtauld Gallery, London.

This is a masterpiece in Monet's late years. A bright and warm color world can be seen in the painting. Its composition is unique. Hallucination-like scenes are the newest artistic achievement of Monet.

schools with their special styles. For example, Jacques-Louis David (French, 1748-1825) and Ingres (French, 1780-1867), the teacher and the student, represented the school of Classicism seeking precision. In the 19th century, De Chirico (French, 1791-1824) and Eugene Delacroix (French, 1798-1863) represented the school of Romanticism with a love for moving and tragic events and good at expressing enthusiasm. Camille Corot (French, 1796-1875), Jean-Francois Millet (French, 1814-1875), Gustave Courbet (French, 1819-1877), and Honore Daumier (French, 1808-1879) represented the school of Realism with natural scenery and social life as their themes. These schools showed their respective excellence. The scene

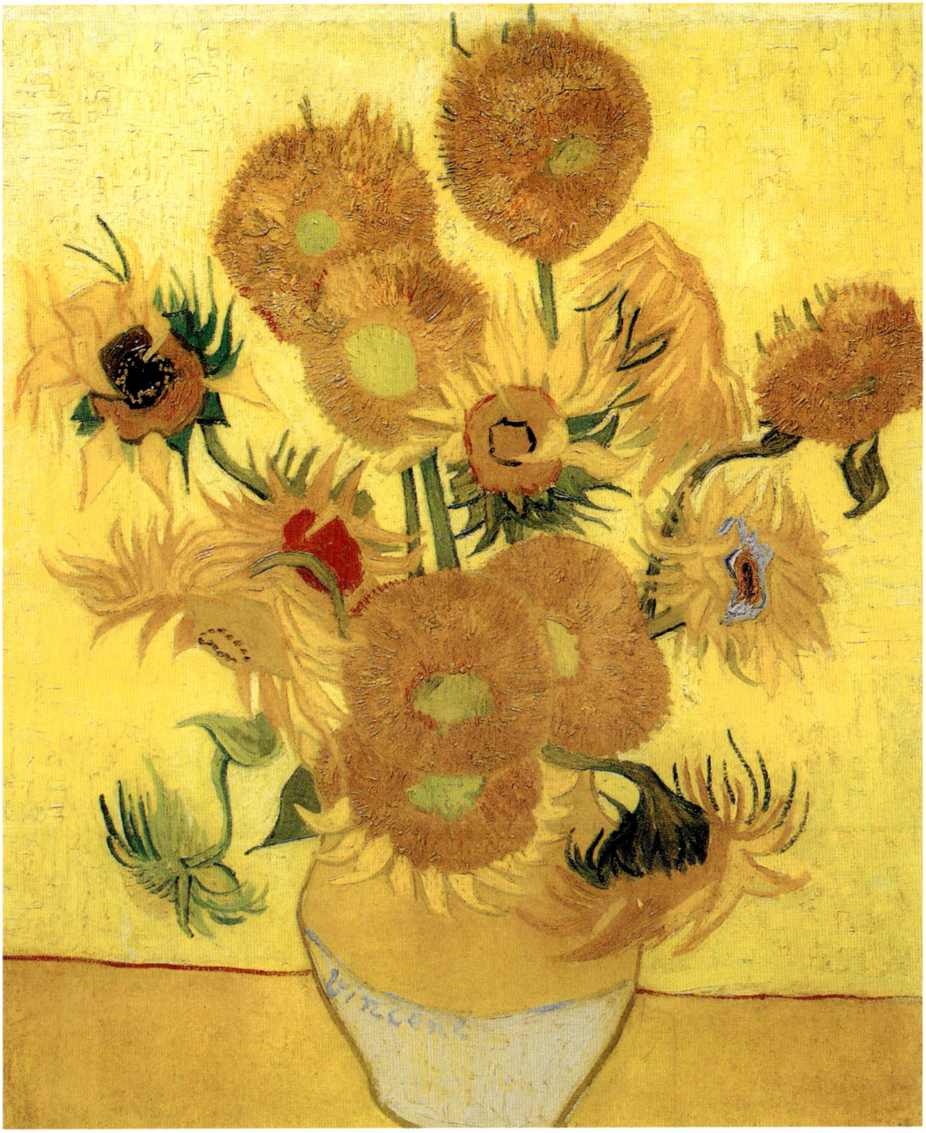

Sunflowers: by Vincent Willem van Gogh of the Netherlands, oil on canvas 95 x 73cm, Preserved in the Van Gogh Museum, Amsterdam.

Sunflowers are the subject of a series of still life paintings by the Dutch painter Vincent van Gogh in Arles. From then on, van Gogh realized that sunflower, the flower of the summer, is a symbol of the sun. Among the Sunflowers paintings are three similar paintings with fifteen sunflowers in a vase, and two similar paintings with twelve sunflowers in a vase. The paintings show sunflowers in all stages of life, from fully in bloom to withering. The paintings were innovative for their use of the yellow spectrum, partly because newly invented pigments made new colours possible.

painted by Camille Corot showing heaven-like poetic flavour; Honore Daumier's cartoons showed a keen-edged sharpness; and Gustave Courbet and Jean-Francois Millet brought a kind sadness to people. In the *Wheat Sifters* by Gustave Courbet the posture of the woman separating the wheat with her straight back and lowered head, makes audiences clearly feel the tiredness in separating wheat and the old sleeping woman beside her further intensified the tiredness, making people want to help her. Jean-Francois Millet's *The Gleaners, The Angelus, Mother and Son*, and *The Sower* all depicted farming lives. The pictures look peaceful but they make

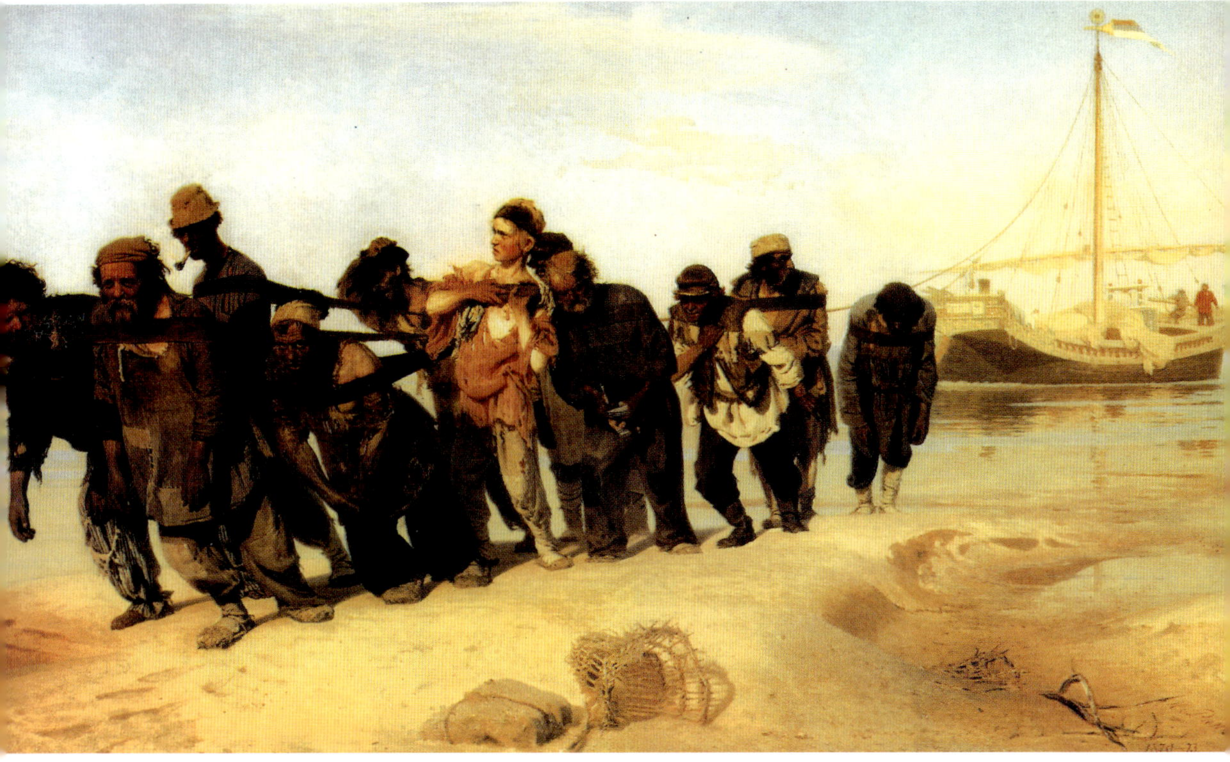

Barge Haulers on the Volga: by Ilya Yefimovich Repin of Russian Empire, 1870-1873, oil on canvas 131.5 x 281cm, Preserved in the Russian Museum, St. Petersburg.

This painting represents a line of barge haulers. This is a typical superior or wiser among the Russian farmers who put up with the flesh and spiritual pain, becoming the leading actor among the barge haulers.

people feel the most touching points in others lives.

After the Renaissance more colours appeared and brown, the main colour during tempera time, was no longer the major colour in paintings. This is owed to scientific development as more and more chemical pigments with brighter colours were synthesized. Until the 19th century the emphasis on colours became more intensive. In the middle and later 19th century Impressionism with all its colours, light and shadow as leading factors came into being guided by Claude Monet (1840-1926). Then Edouard Manet, Auguste Renoir (1841-1919), Camille Pissarro, Alfred Sisley (1839-1899), Georges Seurat, Paul Cezanne, van Gogh, Paul Gauguin, Toulouse Lautrec and Rousseau are also included into the school by later generations. Looking at Sunday Afternoon on the Island of La Grande Jatte by Georges Seurat, you will feel that a colour palette is unwanted, the points of the brushwork create a thoughtful exuberance of vision and colours and the transparency shown in the painting truly interprets the bright and beautiful sunlight.

During the Renaissance a German master Albrecht Durer tried watercolour painting briefly but did not do any further exploration. In the 18th century more and more British landscape painters used watercolours. At first they only applied colours simply to sketches by brush or pen but later they tried to mix colours with cuttlefish juice and finally transparent and clean water colours came into being moving away from the different shades of black colour system. By the end of the 18th century watercolour painting had become increasingly mature and was an independent painting branch keeping up with oil painting. In the 19th century a famous watercolour landscape artist appeared known as J.M.W. Turner.

Generally speaking, after the 18th century western people had a stronger self-awareness and painting had become one of the ways of expressing individualism

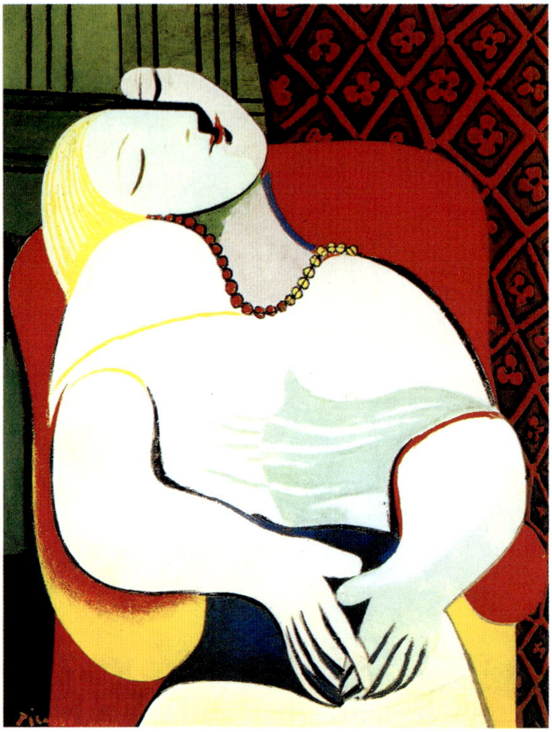

The Dream: Pablo Picasso of Spain, 1932, oil on canvas 130 × 97cm, Private Collection.

The Dream is also called the Women Sleeping in a Red Easy Chair. In this painting, Picasso depicts a female figure with a blend of cubism and neoclassicism styles. It is a masterpiece with the free combination of lines and colors.

and advocating ego. The names of many painters such as (1831-1898), Levitan (1861-1900), (1836-1882), Repin (1844-1930) and Surikov (1848-1916) make people think of the academic, concise and classical aestheticism of painting in Russia, which is a neighbour of Asia, which involves numerous subjects such as historical events, scenes, portraits and people.

The schools emerging in the 20th century completely abandoned the traditional role of painting and only expressed the pure spiritual world. In the early 20th century the famous and influential painting schools included fauve artists represented by Henri Matisse, Cubism represented by Picasso, Dadaism represented by Dali and Abstract Art represented by Wassily Kandinsky.

The changes which have occurred in painting form and content make us realise that painting is no longer the appendage of religion and does not play the role of interpreting religious doctrine any more. It is now closer to real life and shows the affinity of painting.

CHINESE PAINTINGS OF PROPAGANDA, EDUCATION AND SYMPATHY

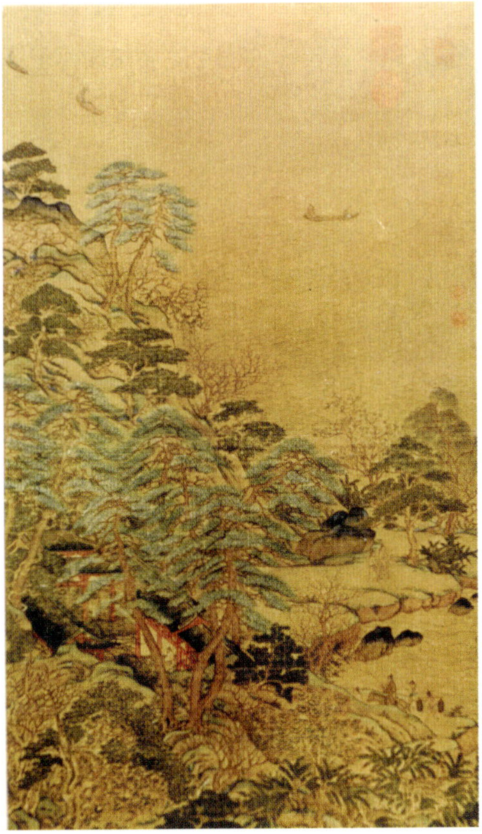

Jiang Fan Lou Ge Tu (Picture of Sail on the River and Pavilion): Scroll, Ink and color on silk 101.9 x 54.7cm, by Li Sixun in the Tang Dynasty, Preserved in the National Palace Museum in Taipei.

The painting style "splendid and magnificent landscape" colors the painting in turquoise and applies yellow to a drawing, showing its resplendence.

From the 3rd to 10th centuries China was in the flourishing age of the Han (206 BC - 220 AD) and Tang (618-907) dynasties when ancient culture in China developed to a peak. Painting was developed independently and before the 6th century landscape and flower-and-bird painting emerged in China paintings alongside figure painting. This means that Chinese painting played the role of cultivating aesthetic interests.

During the Tang Dynasty (618-907) there emerged many landscape painters such as Li Sixun, Li Zhao Dao, Wang Wei, Zhang Zao, Zheng Qian and Wang Mo. Li Sixun and Li Zhao Dao, who were father and son, created the painting style "splendid and magnificent landscape". They gave priority to lines with light-ink strokes and they drew the outline and structure of the objects with lines - even the outline of leaves was line drawn - and then coloured the painting in turquoise. The drawing style was delicate and fresh and the colours were strong and bright.

During the Tang Dynasty (618-907) poetry was very popular and therefore became well developed. At that time people were proficient in using poetry with concise and rhythmic words to sing the praises of the beauty in nature. " The bright moon lifts from the Mountain of Heaven in an infinite haze of cloud and sea" (from *The Moon at the Fortified Pass* by Li Bai), "No dust is raised on the road wet with morning rain, the willows by the hotel look fresh and green (from *A Farewell Song for Yuan Er to Anxi* by Wang Wei), "the full moonlight spreading among the pine trees, the clear spring water flowing on the large stones" (from *Mountain Villa in an Autumn Evening* by Wang Wei) and "Now that the sun has set beyond the

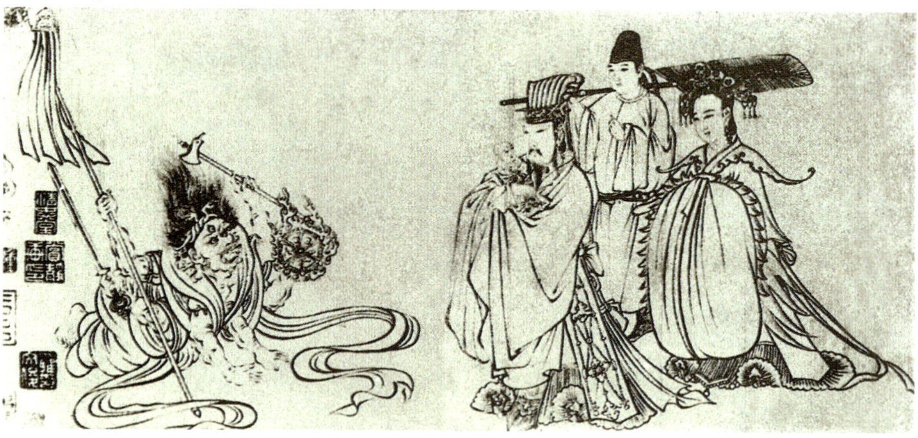

Song Zi Tianwang Tu (God Sending a Son) (Part): Ink on paper 35.7 x 338cm, by Wu Daozi, preserved in the Osaka Museum of Japan.

The painting, divided into three parts, depicts Sakyamuni being born. However, the figures of Suddhodana and Maya are portrayed into the Chinese ancient empress, while gods remain their original expressions in the Buddhist paintings.

western range, Valley after valley is shadowy and dim. And now through the pine-trees comes the moon and the chill of evening, and my ears feel pure with the sound of the wind and water." (From *At the Mountain-lodge of the Buddhist Priest Ye Waiting in Vain for My Friend Ding* by Meng Haoran) are good lines from these poems. The scenes implied by the poetry influenced landscape painting at that time and landscape painters endeavoured to create this poetic atmosphere in their paintings. When it was not enough to express emotion in the painting, a painter could write a poem on the painting combining poetry, calligraphy and painting.

Wang Wei, a famous poet of the Tang Dynasty (618-907), was an all-around master in poetry, calligraphy and painting. If what Li Sixun and his son did is described as "depicting circumstance", then what Wang Wei did in his poetic paintings is described as "creating circumstance." He and other landscape painters adopted lighter ink strokes and explored the possibilities of pen and ink.

Apart from landscape painting great achievements had been made in figure painting during the Tang Dynasty (618-907). For example the following paintings: *Bunian Tu (Receiving the Tibetan Envoy on a Sedan Chair)* by Yan Liben, *Dao Lian Tu (Tang Ladies Preparing Newly Woven Silk)* and *Guo Guo Fu Ren You Chun Tu (After Lady Guo's Spring Tour of the State)* by Zhang Xuan and *Zan Hua Shi Nu Tu (Court Maids Wearing Flowers)* by Zhou Fang are very famous. It is important to mention Wu Daozi, a portrait painter during the Tang Dynasty. He created the special "Chia-like" effect and "wu dai dang feng (the band painted by Wu seems like its flying in wind)" effect, with fluent lines, vigorous strokes and a great proficiency in making garments look like they are naturally flying in the wind. Animal and flower-and-bird painting had developed into independent branches with some advancement. The most famous paintings of this branch that have passed down include *Night-Shining White Hand-scroll* by Han Gan and *The Five Oxen* by Han Huang.

After the rise of literati painting during the Tang Dynasty, (618-907), painting played out another role, that of the self psychological comfort of reclusion. At that time in China, with complete monarchic centralization and a strict concept of hierarchy, the common people could not exercise any power on the fate and development of the country and even had no say. Just because people did not have any right to say anything did not mean people were without individual points of view. In this sense many literati painters used the aid of paintings to express their thoughts and some completely lost their interest in current politics and expressed their loftiness and otherworldly thoughts by their paintings.

After the 10th century the role of Chinese painting witnessed no great change. Its basic role was promoting religious concepts (Buddhism and other Chinese native religious such as Taoism and Confucianism) but it also promoted the idea of royal domination, the self psychological comfort of reclusion and aesthetic sentiment.

Painting witnessed a complete change in style while developing during the Five Dynasties, (907-960) and the Song Dynasty, (960-1279). The main achievement during the Tang Dynasty, (618-907), was to make painting break away from its attached position as ser mon and illustration to become a specific and pure art category which was divided into several branches. Let us look at the style of painting during the Tang Dynasty, especially landscapes. In both "depicting"and "creating circumstances" objects were represented in the distance with a completely objective expression. During the Song Dynasty compared to the Tang Dynasty, the whole style of painting became much leaner and a subjective expression with ego appeared combining ego into objects and trying to clear up the distance. In terms of

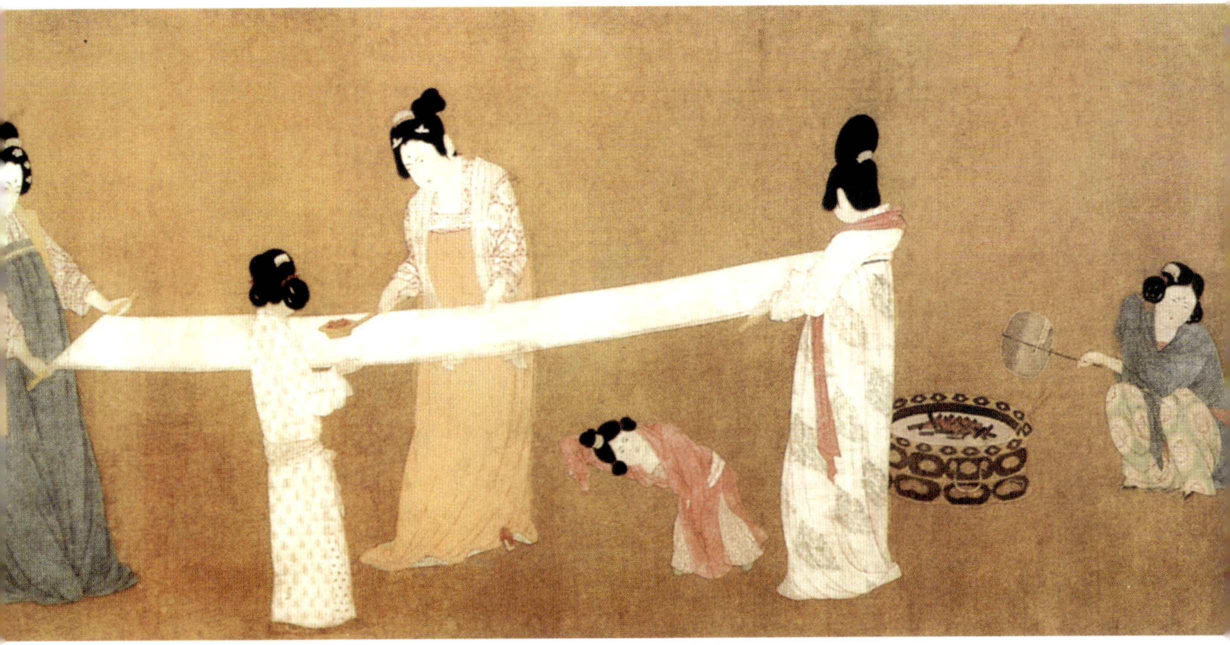

Dao Lian Tu (Tang Ladies Preparing Newly Woven Silk) (Part): By Zhang Xuan in Tang Dynasty (Copy in the Song Dynasty), Ink and color on silk 37 x 147cm, Preserved by Museum of Fine Arts, Boston, the US.

This painting depicts the women in the Palace smashing the white silk and weaving. With simple, bright color, it shows the flourishing atmosphere in the palace during the flourishing age.

technology, Li Gonglin in the Song Dynasty kept improving representation by lines and made line drawing into an independent branch; Liang Kai specialized in subtle changes of ink colour and created the ink and brush style of painting known as (xieyi). In landscape painting more attention was paid to changes of vigour in the style and ink colour, more kinds of light-ink strokes appeared and the ink brush painting style of landscapes came into being. In the Song Dynasty there also appeared such independent painting branches as "ink bamboo" and "ink plum blossom". Plum blossom, orchid, bamboo and chrysanthemum are representations of excellent quality in eyes of Chinese literati, i.e. aloofness, pride, elegance, humility, honesty and not always following what was normal.

The Han nationality has the largest population in China and its economy,

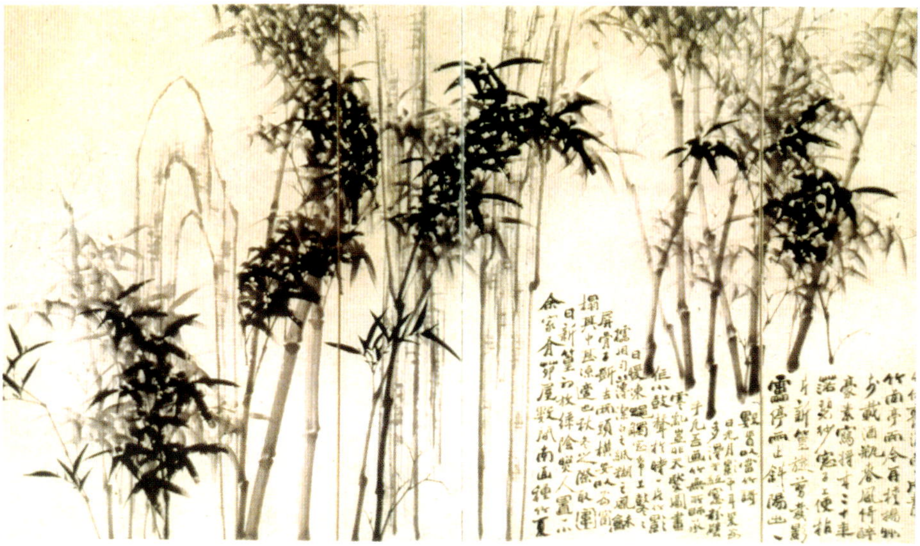

Black Bamboo: 119.2 x 235.5cm, by Zheng Banqiao in the Qing Dynasty,
Preserved in Tokyo National Museum.

science and technology and culture are comparatively stronger than other ethnic minorities. The ruling classes of past dynasties were mostly Han people. Then a change occurred in the Yuan Dynasty (1271-1368) when Mongol people occupied the sovereignty of China and it was a hard fact for many Han people to accept. Their self-esteem was challenged and impacted seriously but there was nothing they could do. So they selected art to escape from reality. Such psychology of literati was represented by placing their feelings on paintings of landscapes, nature, flowers, birds, insects and fish. So during the Yuan Dynasty the landscape, bamboo, plum blossom and flower-and-bird paintings were comparatively well developed. The landscape painting of the Yuan Dynasty was characterized by brighter, cleaner and loftier scenes than that of the Song Dynasty (960-1279). This served to place their spirituality into the paintings and express obscurely their dissatisfaction of reality. This was especially outstanding in works by Ni Zan. Their attitude to painting was "freehand sketches aim at expressing their emotions in hearts instead of seeking for similarity in form." With such a background there were fewer figure paintings, more religious and fable themes and the appearances of objects were often transformed in order to attach importance to the figures' personalities in the paintings of the Yuan Dynasty.

During the Ming Dynasty (1368-1644) there appeared the Wumen School and the Zhe School of landscape paintings represented by Shenzhou, Wen Zhengming and Dai Jin respectively. The famous flowers-and-birds painting masters included Lin Liang, Lu Ji, Bian Wenjin and Zhou Zhimian. The figure painting masters include Qiu Ying and Chen Hongshou. Although there appeared many great painters during the Ming Dynasty traditional Chinese painting witnessed no outstanding innovations during this dynasty.

The Qing Dynasty (1644-1911) was another time when China was under the domination of an ethnic minority. The whole Han literati once again went into negative emotions. In painting, besides the fullness of reclusive emotions, there appeared a differentiation in

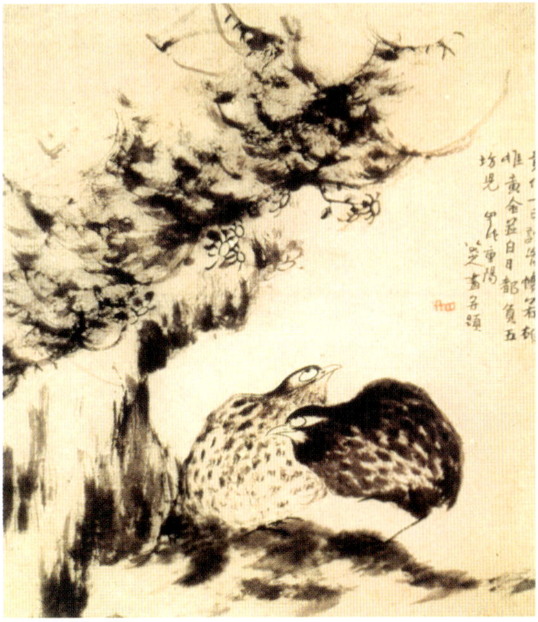

An Wan Tie Yi: 31.7 x 27.7cm, on paper, by Zhu Da in the Qing Dynasty, Private collection in Kyoto, Japan

Zhu Da is also called the Eight Great Hermits. The brushwork of the eyes of the birds in the painting is Zhu Da's characteristics, showing his unruly character and dissatisfaction with the rule of the Qing court.

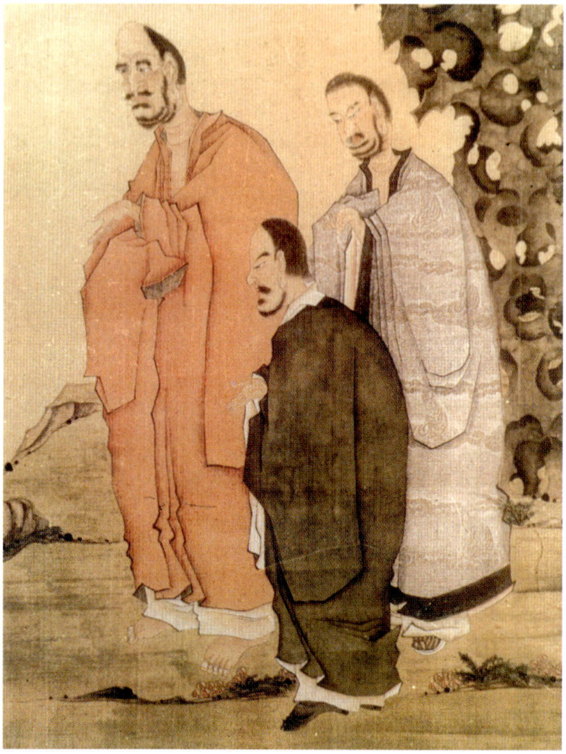

Lian Chi Yin Hua Tu Zhou (Scroll of the Lotus Pond) (Part): Ink and color on silk, by Chen Hongshou in the Ming Dynasty. Preserved in the National Palace Museum in Taipei.

The figures in the painting include Amitabha, Mahasthamaprapta and Avalokitesvara. Chen Hongshou's paintings feature strange figures and rigidity, being used as

techniques. This school, represented by the Four Wangs i. e. Wang Shimin, Wang Jian, Wang Hui, and Wang Yuanqi, advocated following the ancient styles and maintaining the original features of traditional painting. The school represented by the Eight Great Hermits and Shi Tao extended their dissatisfaction on the occupation of the country to betrayal of the restraint by traditional techniques. They argued that technique was only a tool and people did not have to follow a certain technique as long as they could express themselves clearly.

After the 20th century, with the introduction of western science and culture, people's concepts are increasingly combined with western styles and painting follows the example of the west in the aspects of both techniques and aesthetics.

As to the role of painting, it is necessary to mention another kind of painting, Chinese folk painting. Such painting had almost no relation with the art society but was/is an integral part of regional life. This art's main role was of praying to heaven for peace and happiness. Generally speaking the Han people are a group of indrawn people and do not like to express their thoughts directly so they created many signs and symbols. For example the guava fruit has many seeds and Chinese people use it to imply giving birth to many children; also in Chinese the word for "fish" has a similar pronunciation with the words "surplus" and "richness" so the painting of fish is used to imply the hope of surplus money and a rich life. In folk art in China there are many such images wishing good in all aspects of life such as the guava fruit, fish, the magpie and the lotus. In Chinese folk painting two great generals of the Tang Dynasty (618-907), Qin Qiong and Yuchi Gong are also painted or pasted on doorways, one on the left and one on the right, as door-gods to protect the house.

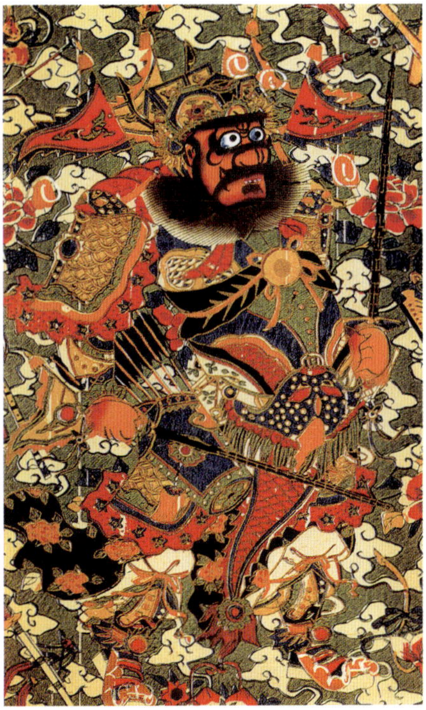
Yuchi Gong

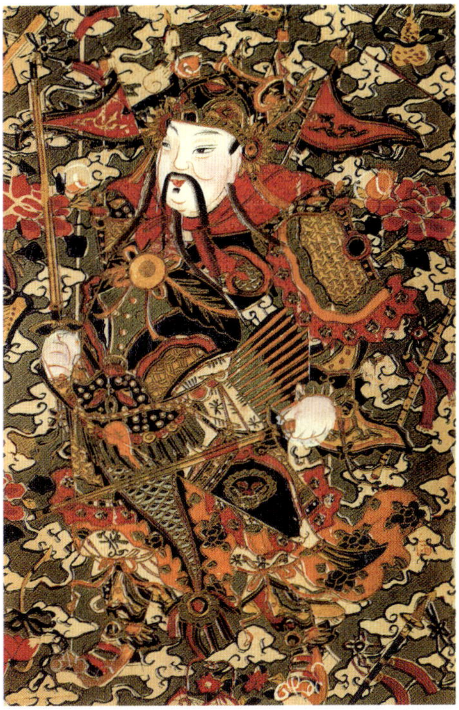
Qin Qiong

Folk painting also filled the role that literati painting did not, recording historical events by figures with swords and horses, such as the figure paintings of Qin Qiong and Yuchi Gong. According to legend, Emperor Taizong of the Tang Dynasty (618-907), Li Shimin (599-649), killed many people in his process of seizing power. After he ascended the throne his health was very poor and he often had dreams that ghosts were throwing bricks and tiles and crying aloud in his bedroom. Unable to bear such torture, Li Shimin called in his generals and civil officials to discuss countermeasures. His generals recommended Qin Qiong, a marshal with supreme skill in Wushu and the great general, Yuchi Gong, to guard his palace on both sides every night. After that he passed his nights peacefully. As time passed, thinking Qin Qiong and Yuchi Gong were tired working days and nights, Li Shimin ordered the palace painters to draw their pictures with their soldiers complete with intimidating expressions, fierce eyes and whip and mace in their hands. The pictures were hung on both sides of the palace doors. From then on all evil spirits and ghosts disappeared. This method was followed by later generations and Qin Qiong and Yuchi Gong became the most popular door-gods in folk history and they are still popular today.

If we say that western painting enters man's mundane life deeper and deeper from a religious circle, then the development of Chinese painting is a religion by itself: literary people placed their aloof, lofty and reclusive emotions in their painting and the common people placed their expectations for safety and happiness in their folk painting.

Chapter II: The Directness of the Hunting Style and the Restraint of the Farming Style

——A Comparison of Emotions between Chinese and Western Paintings.

When we look at the figures in western paintings there are more and more smiles. The figures in Western paintings show abundant and directly expressed emotions such as happiness, anger, grief, joy, and terror. When we look at the figures in Chinese paintings it is hard to see a smile. If you observe more carefully you will find very few figures in Chinese paintings give out body language. Most of them are restrained and their emotions are contained but not shown in the pictures. In this aspect western paintings attach importance to the expression of sensibility while Chinese paintings are inclined towards the expression of sense. In fact the expression of sense in Chinese paintings also has sensibility while the expression of sensibility in western paintings contains sense.

Directness and Restraint

A man's early life experience influences and even decides his character and way of thinking and doing after he becomes an adult. The way early humans lived also influenced profoundly their way of thinking and doing and their way of expressing emotion in later life and hence in different civilizations you get different cultural developments.

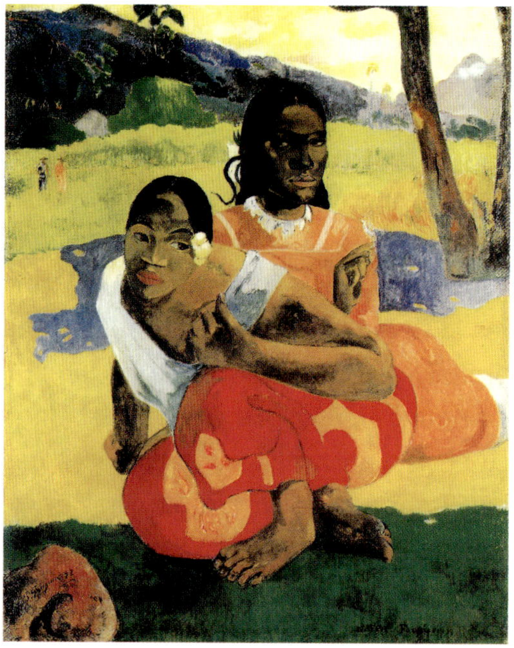

When Will You Marry?: by Paul Gauguin of France, 1892, Oil on canvas 105 x 77.5cm, Preserved in the Rudolf Staechelin Family Foundation, Basel.

The title of this painting is directly reflected in the painting. Its colors are purer, with red, yellow, green and black being used, showing the healthy complexion of the female, red copper.

The earliest humans lived in similar ways - they were hunter gatherers (hunting animals and collecting fruits and wild plants). Due to different geographical and climatic conditions the style and manner of living of the later eastern and western people witnessed considerable differences.

Europe is located to the north

of Latitude 35 degrees and most of it belongs to the temperate zone. It is mostly flat or plains terrain with occasional mountains. There are many rivers spread over it. About 39 percent of the total area of Europe (including Russia) is forest. The western coast of Europe boasts some of the best fisheries in the world. The coastline area of its fisheries occupies 32 percent of the total fishing area along all coasts worldwide. These natural conditions allowed the western people to keep easily to their original living habits as the large-area forests are suitable for hunting and fishing was easy near the coast and rivers.

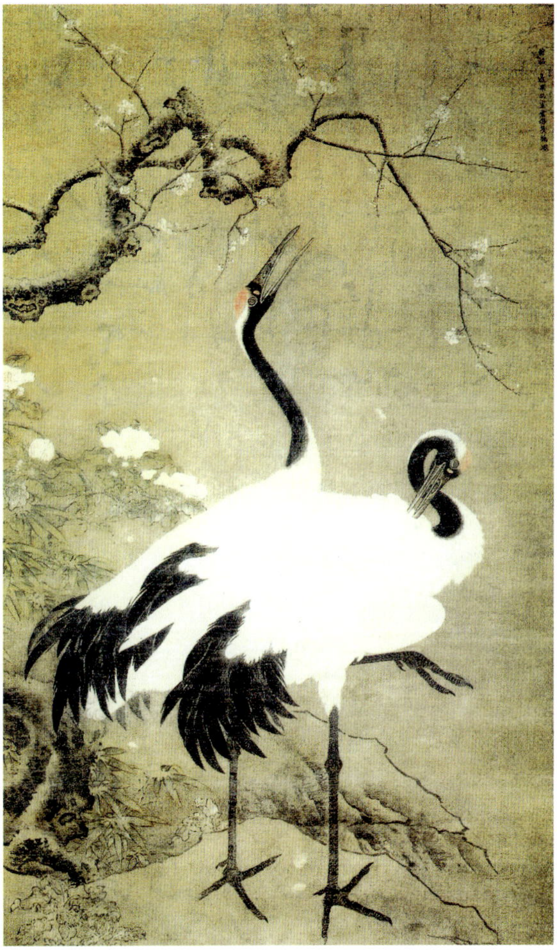

Xue Mei Shuang He Tu (Picture of Wintersweet in Snow and Double Cranes): By Bian Jingzhao in the Ming Dynasty, Ink and color on silk156 x 91cm, Preserved in the Guangdong Provincial Museum.

The Crane is an immortal bird symbolizing luck and longevity in Chinese traditional concept.

Such a lifestyle made the ancestors of western people possess the more distinctive features of flesh eating people. They became stronger in the course of hunting the animals and eating their flesh. As a result their nervous systems became fully developed and their psychology and intelligence were more aggressive, so they became a behaviouristic people characterized by direct thoughts and actions and comparatively direct emotional expression.

Their drawings are all direct and clear at a glance and people's emotions are expressed by their faces.

The Central Plain area of China occupies a relatively larger area where the four seasons are separated from each other clearly, the ground is suitable for planting and irrigation is relatively convenient. So people gradually abandoned their original hunting life quite easily and turned to develop a farming lifestyle. Farming is not as quick and easy as hunting in supplying food and people need to wait for the changes in seasons and the growing of plants patiently.

Such waiting hardened people's temperament and gradually cultivated a lot of patience. People became less and less self-determined and aggressive in the course of relying on nature and they developed a more vegetarian lifestyle. They became mild mannered and conceded easily and their self-protection consciousness was strong while their attacking consciousness was weak. Due to the instinct of self protection and preservation most of their deeds were not apparent or direct but became indirect and restrained.

The garden architecture of China is a vivid portrait of Chinese psychology: it is impossible for visitors to see the end, at a glance, of the small bridges, running rivers and zigzag winding corridors.

Painting is similar in that it is hard to find the psychology of the painters after a glance at most of the literati paintings.

SENSE AND SENSIBILITY

When we look at the figures in western paintings there are more and more smiles starting with the restrained smile of Mona Lisa. All of the figures in *The Gypsy Woman* by Hales, *The Feast* of Bacchus by Diego Velazquez, *Mme de Pompadour*

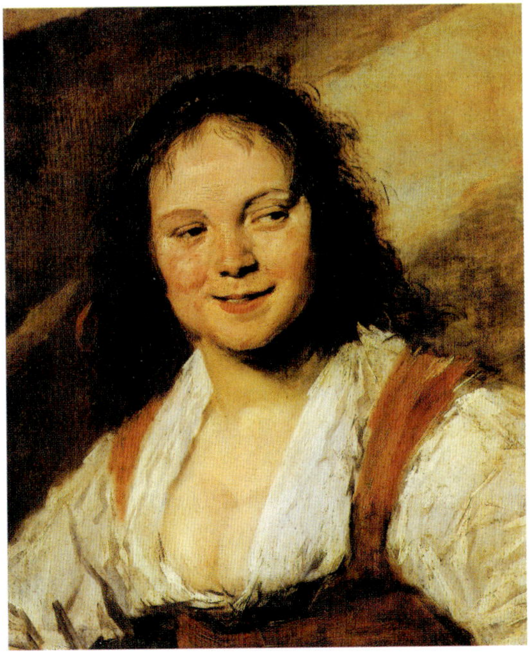

The Gypsy Woman by Hales

The painter used the bright brush stroke to reinforce the expressive force. The figure in the painting is a representative of the free and zestful Gypsy girls. The civilian blood of the girl is well and truly depicted by the painter with the proficient skills and warm tones.

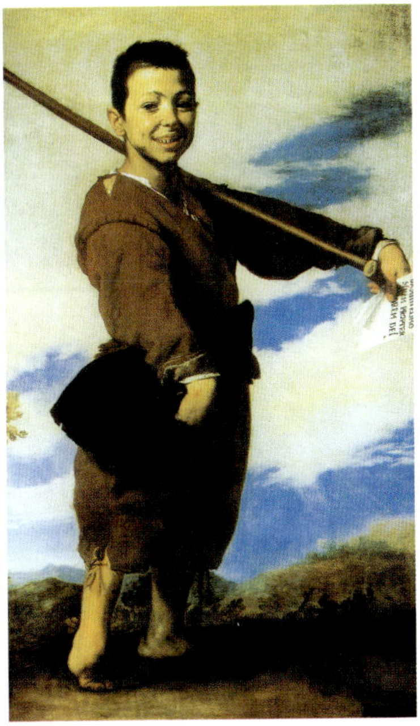

The lame Boy: 1642, Oil on canvas, by Jusepe de Ribera of Spain.

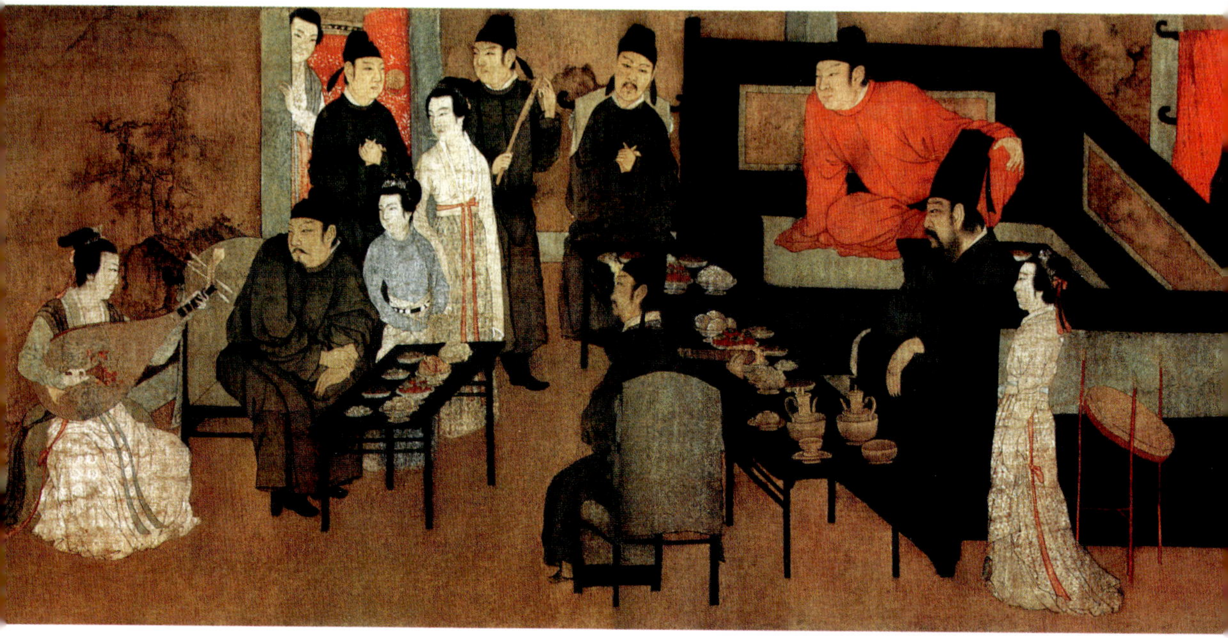

Han Xizai Yeyan Tu (the Night Revels of Han Xizai) (Part): Ink and color on silk 28.7 × 335.5cm, by Gu Hongzhong in the Five Dynasties (907-960).

In the painting Han Xizai Yeyan Tu (Night Revels of Han Xizai) set in a home with a banquet and singing and dancing, it should be very joyful but the picture again reflects quietness.

by Etienne-Maurice Falconet and *The Shrimp Girl* by William Hogarth have vivid and touching smiles and even the lame child under the brushwork of Ribena in *The Lame Boy* has a brilliant smile. The figures in western paintings show abundant and directly expressed emotions such as happiness, anger, grief, joy, and terror.

When we look at the figures in Chinese paintings it is hard to see a smile even of a woman. From the Picture of *Nu Shi Zhen (Admonition on Female Officials)*, *Lie Nu Tu (Women Died in Defence of their Honour and Chastity)* and *Luoshen Fu Tu (The Nymph of the Luo River)* by Gu Kaizhi to *Picture of the Emperors of Past Dynasties* and *Bunian Tu (Receiving the Tibetan Envoy on a Sedan Chair)* by Yan Liben to *Dao Lian Tu (Tang Ladies Preparing Newly Woven Silk)* and *Guo Guo Fu*

Ren You Chun Tu (After Lady Guo's Spring Tour of the State) by Zhang Xuan to *Zan Hua Shi Nv Tu (Court Maids Wearing Flowers)* by Zhou Fang to *Song Zi Tianwang Tu (God Sending a Son)* by Wu Daozi and to *Han Xizai Yeyan Tu (Night Revels of Han Xizai)* by Gu Hongzhong and to the figures by Fei Danxu and Ren Xiong during the Qing Dynasty (1644-1911) we can hardly see a smile. The Buddha figures in religious mural paintings have quite a few kindly smiles. If you observe more carefully you will find very few figures in Chinese paintings give out body language. Most of them are restrained and their emotions are contained but not shown in the pictures.

In this aspect western paintings attach importance to the expression of sensibility while Chinese paintings are inclined towards the expression of sense.

In fact the expression of sense in Chinese paintings also has sensibility while the expression of sensibility in western paintings contains sense.

First let's look at western paintings. In traditional representational paintings, no matter how abundant and touching the emotions are that are shown by the figures in the paintings, it is a kind of realistic visual representation completely persisting in the copying of objects with their exact proportion and structure. The artist has to be rational while expressing his skill in terms of precision of shape and authenticity of colour. During the Impressionist period the brushwork with various brilliant colours showed the painters' rational analysis on colour, chroma and colour differences. The Impressionist Paul Cezanne visually showed his sense by his paintings. In his work, *The Cardplayers*, the postures and expressions of the figures are dispassionate and the colour and circumstances also show sense and the basic geometric composition can be seen in the figure's structure. In Cubism the paintings are further flooded with a sense of structural reorganization. The Abstract school brings the role of sense into full play.

Now let's look at the Chinese paintings. In Chinese paintings it is hard to see any smiles on the figures, there are not many body language touches and those that are there are restrained. The treatment of emotions, containing but not showing, should be the real portrait of Chinese life because in reality the Chinese have maintained restraint until the middle and latter part of the 20th century. They were not good at expressing their happiness, anger, sorrow and joy and other emotions directly. They were ashamed to tell you directly what made them feel happy or unhappy. They felt embarrassed to show their emotions on their faces. They even felt embarrassed to embrace their own parents and families. When they met others, they would not embrace or shake hands but bow with hands folded in front and even kowtow to elder people. In the 20th century the only physical touch made by Chinese people was shaking hands when meeting others. So they are a race of people shy in their hearts. But their tendency to being shy results in abundant and minute emotions. Like water, a man's emotion needs a channel for running way when it is ready to overflow so they

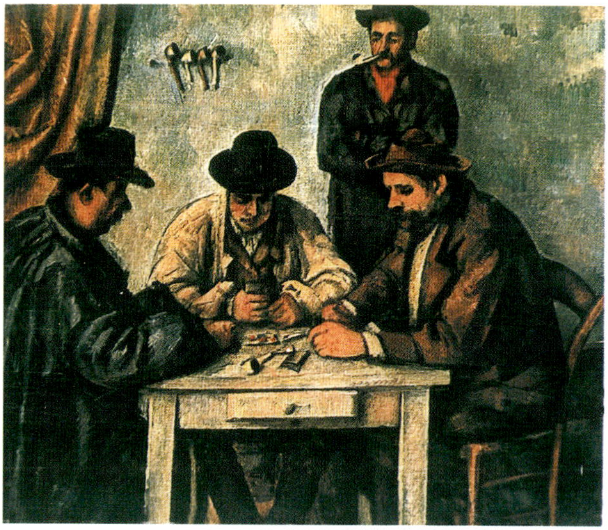

The Cardplayers: 1890-1892, Oil on canvas 65 × 81cm, by Paul Cezanne of France, Private Collection in New York

It is remarkable how thoroughly interesting is this perfectly legible picture, how rich in effective inventions of color and form. The painter is more interested in expressing the abstract meaning of his painting than the story.

select such ways as exchanging feelings and allegory to express their emotions. Therefore, people can understand why there are so many allegorical ways in China, such as simile and metaphor. The objects for people to exchange feelings are often mountains, stones and trees in nature, so landscape painting is very developed in China and their emotions are mostly expressed by mountains, stones and trees.

In Chinese painting nature is often personalized. In *Jie Zi Yuan (The Mustard Seed Garden)*, there is a passage about painting a pine tree, "a pine tree seems like a man of moral integrity. His posture looks like a low-lying dragon trying to please a valley but like a dragon it has a dignity and awe and prestige in its heart that others cannot intrude into." This means that if a person painting a pine tree can feel the inside bearing of the pine tree, he can paint an unusual pine tree.

Even facing non living stone, Chi-

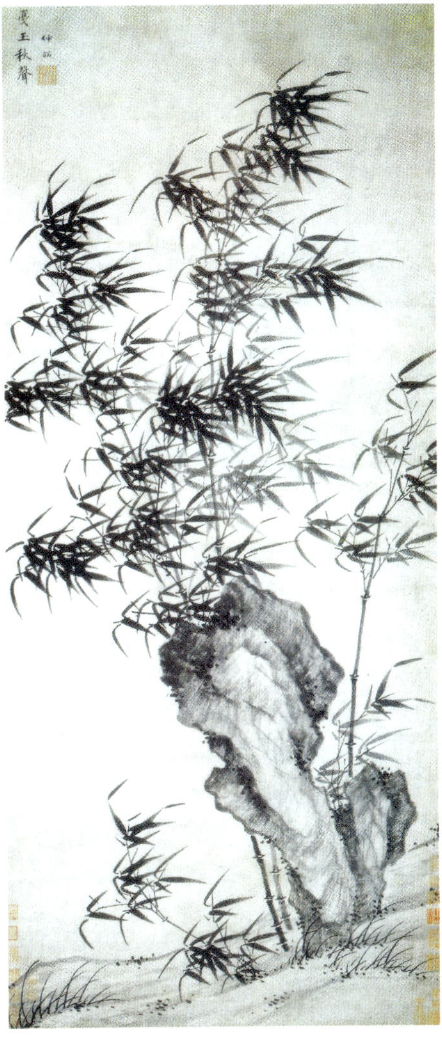

Ga Yu Qiu Sheng Tu (Picture of Jade and Sound in Autumn): In the Ming Dynasty, Scroll, Ink on paper 151 x 63.7cm, Preserved in the Shanghai Museum.

This painting depicts a stone erecting on a slope and a cluster of thin bamboos joggling in the autumn winds. The painter vividly represents a ragged space with dense and light inks and impersonal simulation, successfully creating a beautiful and lifelike artistic world.

nese painters can view it as a living thing when painting it. In traditional Chinese painting, importance is attached to "living" when painting stones. In the eyes of Chinese painters, stones can be divided into two main categories: those surrounding mountains and those close to water. Those surrounding mountains are compared to the mountains' grandchildren and those close to water are compared to the water's children. The stones have consanguinity with the mountains or water nearby. Some artists often paint stones as the nose tip of a man and the painted stones are full of expression.

From the above the observation about Chinese painting does not emphasize especially the relations in space but the whole shape and the relations expressed - what are the postures held by the objects and what are the relations expressed and they are characterized by personalization and having emotions.

In this way Chinese people personalize the objects in nature and place their feelings on them to lead off the various emotions in their hearts. So it can be said that Chinese painting is rational in appearance but expresses sensibility in nature.

Objective and Subjective

Once we can possess feelings and are able to express feelings, man could "feel the sight of certain things stir up his feelings." Some people would record the things and scenes that stir up their feelings and their memory, their mental associations and excited emotions in words, paintings and music. Hence we can find art works that create a sympathetic response. Such a deed is to record a reality: a real scene, a real emotion and a real feeling and thought. They would not add too many subjective elements and would stick by records even when expressing their emotions. This is the objective expression, i.e. depicting circumstance. It should be said that western painting tends to depict circumstance with objective expression. Painters would prefer expressing their sights and feelings objectively and realistically not caring much about others' opinions.

Philosophers like to define philosophy as pondering over the pondering of life and they always think only rational people like to think and are good at thinking. They think western people are more rational and better at thinking than Chinese people and western philosophy is more developed than Chinese philosophy. Many Chinese people also concluded from Chinese and western dramas and stories that western people possess more philosophic characters than Chinese people. Western literature and films have mostly tragic endings, leaving more thoughts and self-reflection to the audience. Chinese literature and films have mostly happy endings and audiences feel comfortable and delighted and there are fewer thoughts and self-reflections. But this is only an appearance.

In fact life is always permeated with Chinese philosophy. Chinese people live after thinking, and their philosophical concepts are their living concepts and vice versa. Such phrases as "taking things as they come" and "being content with one's lot to feel constantly happy" look ordinary but they are actually the philosophical and living concepts achieved by generations of Chinese after the accumulation of living experiences and repeated thinking.

Chinese people pay attention to "taking things as they come", i.e. advocating that people should adjust their psychology and deeds according to circumstances, make themselves suit the surrounding circumstances and then they can lead a comfortable life. They pay attention to "being content with one's lot to feel happy constantly," meaning to be content with life at present and not to hold too many hopes and then they will feel happy for a long time in their hearts. Such concepts make people feel that Chinese people have a low key living attitude. In fact it is an appearance. Apparently, such expressions are the Chinese people's sayings for self-discipline but actually they are aimed at others. Chinese people often like to put their thoughts and achievements to others to get a sympathetic response and even hope others hold the same concepts as themselves, so Chinese people hold a stronger subjectivity.

The subjectivity of Chinese people is represented in painting by being good at "creating circumstance" - painters often blend their thoughts and feelings into paintings and add much more subjective elements.

Some people may say that western painters also add their feelings to paintings,

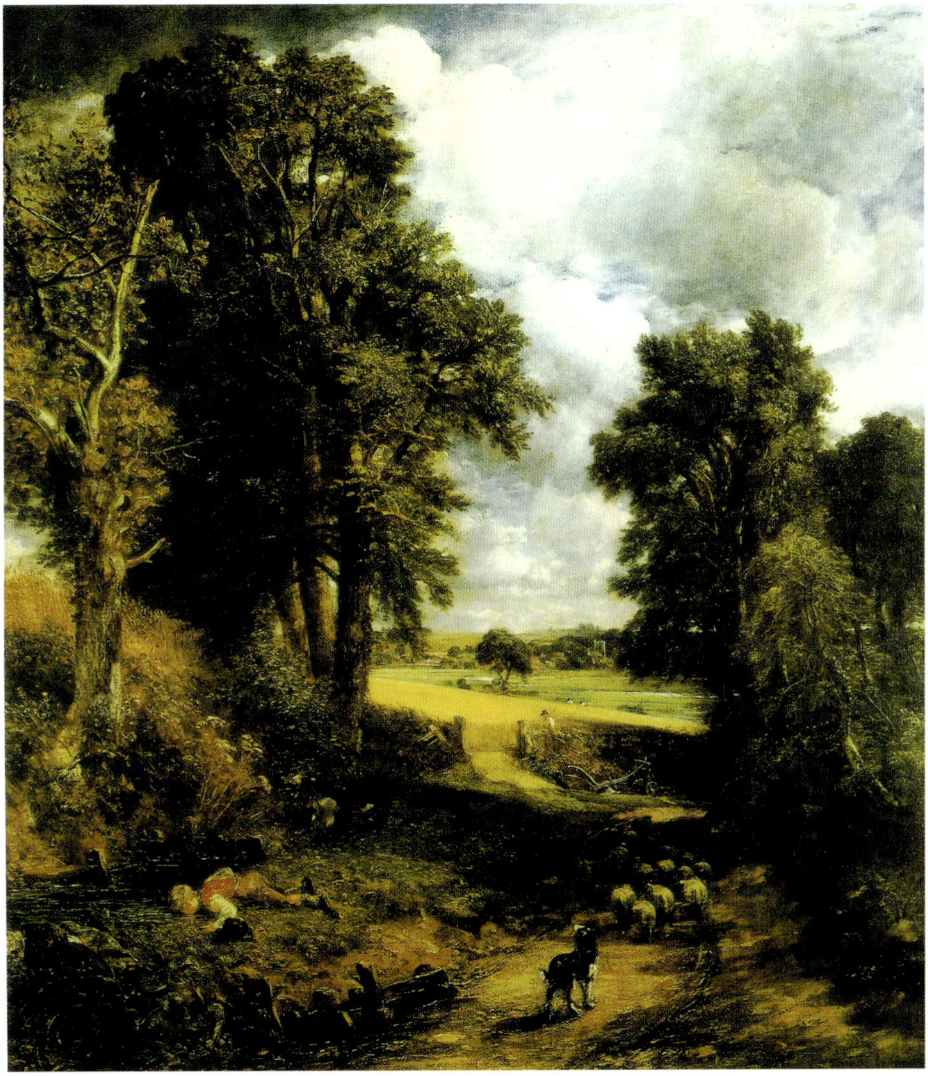

The Wheat Field: By English John Constable, 1826, oil on canvas 143 x 122cm, Preserved in the National Gallery.

This painting takes the green as the main tone. John Constable depicts the green in the different depths of a scene with different Hue.

don't they? Actually western painters use a different way to blend their feelings into paintings from those used by Chinese painters. Their subjective elements are only represented by the extracted objects, i.e. they would extract the objects that stir up their feelings, but when representing them, they basically stick by the objects. There will be little difference between their work and real objects, so compared to subjective elements, there are more objective elements. Of course, this only aims at realistic painting.

It is hard to contrast Chinese paintings with objects in reality especially landscape paintings. In the west landscape painters mostly set up their easels on the spot and paint from nature - put the sight truly to pictures to the best of their abilities. It is different in China. The Chinese painting tools are not as easy to carry as those in the west, so Chinese landscape painters mostly remember the

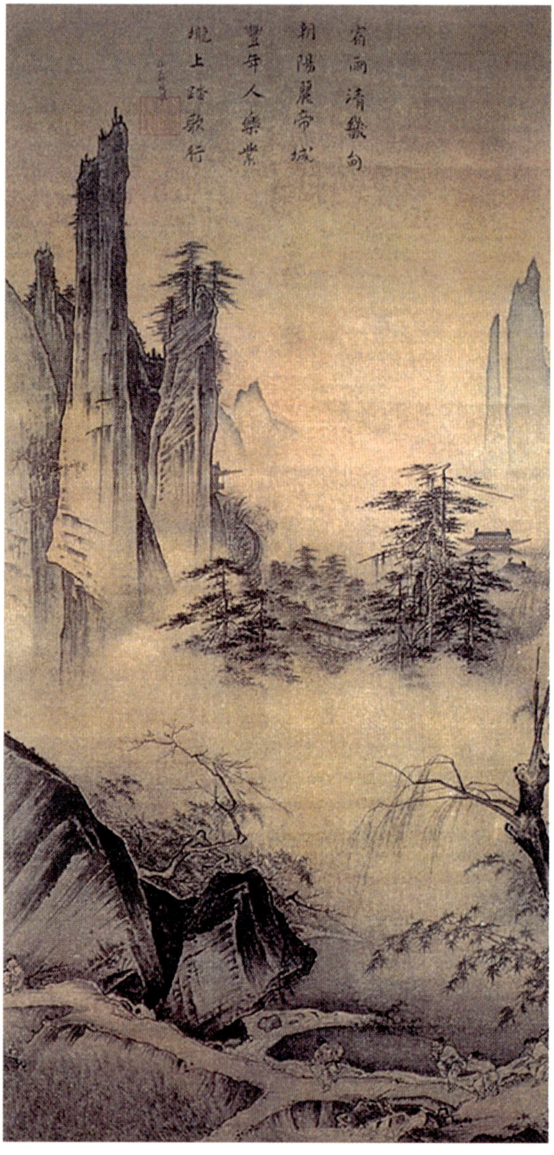

Ta Ge Tu Zhou: By Ma Yuan in the Southern Song Dynasty (1127-1279), Ink and color on silk 192.5 x 111cm, Preserved in the Palace Museum in Beijing.

The painter Ma Yuan likes to represent a corner of a landscape, in which the scenery is very simple, hence the name Ma Yijiao (a corner) in the history of Chinese painting!

scenes and start to paint after returning to their studios. It is impossible for painters to remember all the details exactly and they can only remember the most touching and impressive parts. It means that Chinese landscape paintings need a long time from actually seeing to actually painting. During this time the true objects experience screening and processing by feelings. The attractive parts are intensified and enlarged by memory and those parts having nothing to do with feelings are weakened and forgotten. Then the pictures on paper are different from reality. The true objects are reorganized in the painting according to aesthetic rules, after the painters' subjective adding and deleting. Structure, contrast between entirety and details and the proportional distribution of black, white and grey are arranged rationally. So Chinese paintings show a strong subjective flavour: some are lofty, beautiful or far away... The atmosphere created in the paintings easily attracts people's attention. When thinking over it carefully, people will find no shortcomings: the structure on the whole does not breach the reality, the concrete growing tendency of mountains is correct, the geological structure and texture of the mountains is vivid and so are the trees. Then you cannot help gasping in admiration: your feelings about the landscape are represented concisely and clearly by painters who abstract the kernel of true life and do their artistic process on it. Such art cannot be replaced by photographs or other forms of art.

Restriction and Opening

Painting is a free and unstrained art and every one can express his individuality and thoughts at random by painting and painting is also an art restricted by nature, materials and artificial elements.

First, painting is restricted by nature. The regional and geographical climate, scenery and products have impacts on the local lifestyle and this specific lifestyle results in relevant ways of thinking and doing. For example, unsettled nomads who depended on herding and hunting usually had an aggressive personality. Settled people depending on farming had a comparatively stable way of life, so they only hoped to safeguard their vested interests. Moreover, they had no experience of continuously moving around as exercise and, as a result, they were much weaker than nomads, so it is rarely heard of that farming communities expanded and invaded others. The material and physical conditions decided that they only needed to safeguard and not to attack. For natural and artificial disasters the Chinese people, the majority of whom came from a farming culture, brought their patience into full play and created a set of theories to obtain psychological comfort. For example, Laozi had a vivid metaphor: "Facing a strong wind, the big, strong tree stands upright and it is broken by a gust of instantaneous strong wind; the weak and hollow reed cleverly bends down when a gust of wind comes and when the wind is gone it is still safe". The apparently tall and strong tree lost its life as it did not know to adapt itself to the circumstances, while the naturally weak reed protected its life as it knew how to protect itself. The idea of retreat and acclimation has had a profound impact on Chinese painters and on their thoughts, aesthetics, deeds and painting styles. Some literati painters with great artistic accomplishments in the end led reclusive or monarchic lives and there are many master pieces praising hermits in the history of Chinese painting. Fundamentally speaking, the natural living conditions cultivate their retreat and acclimation.

Painting is restricted by artificial elements. Modern painting in China is similar to that in the west and some of it is even more excessive than western paintings in the aspect of vanguard. But in ancient times Chinese painting was restricted by various etiquettes and regulations. The criteria in everyday life for ancient Chinese people might have been stricter than the etiquette learned by stewards today. From birth children were indoctrinated with all the etiquette and regulations by those adults who earnestly practiced what they were teaching and gradually they cultivated some customs. Can you imagine seeing smiling figures in mainstream paintings during the age when women could not smile at random (they could not expose their teeth when smiling and smiling at random was viewed as flirtatious) and both men and women could not easily show their happiness, anger, sorrow and joy (showing at random was viewed as a sign of instability) ? In ancient China it was forbidden to expose any part of the body even the teeth and if even the sleeves of a man and a woman touched together, it would be viewed as impurity - "men and women would be viewed as losing their chastity if their sleeves were touched together or if they roll up their sleeves." Naked body portraiture which could be seen in western painting was also a taboo in traditional Chinese paintings. The regional

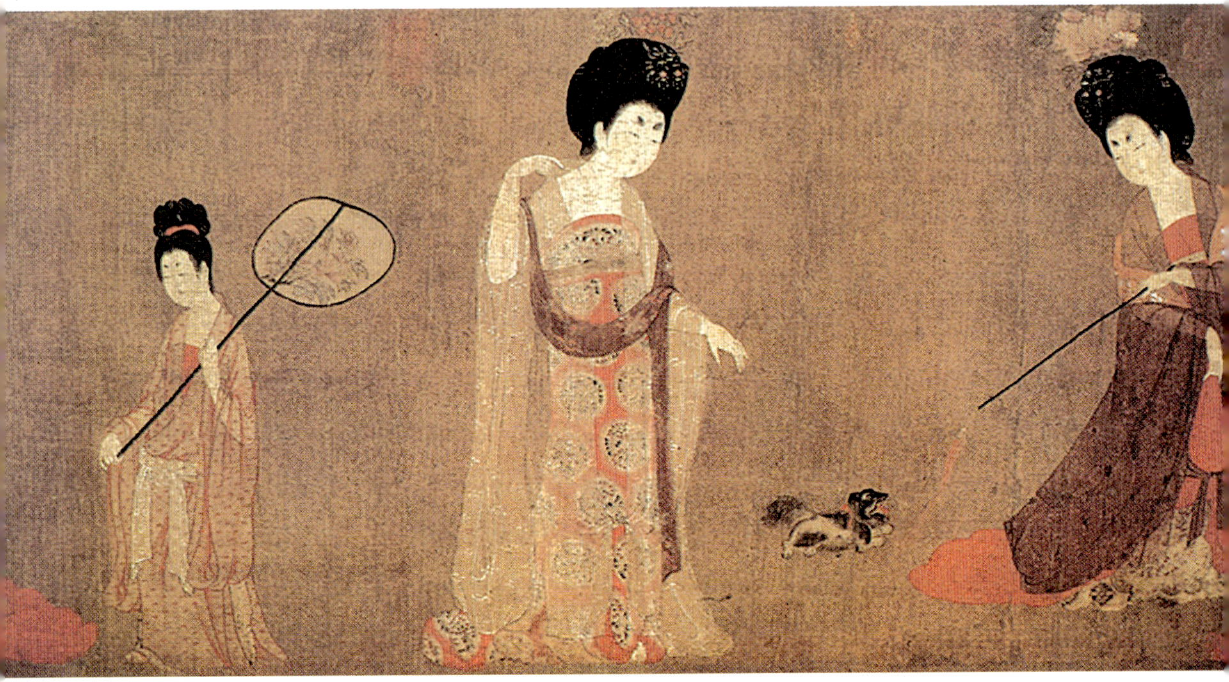

Zan Hua Shi Nu Tu (Court Maids Wearing Flowers) (Part): Zhou Fang in the Tang Dynasty, Hanging scroll, Ink and color on silk 46 x 180cm, Preserved in the Liaoning Provincial Museum.

The painting, which originally was like one in the screen, and later mounted into a horizontal scroll, depicted high-ranking court maids playing in the palace. The women have the hair worn in a bun or coil and clothes made of silk.

customs and culture made it hard for painting themes to break through the very strict limitations at that time.

It is necessary to explain one thing. Few of the figures in Chinese literati paintings have smiles but why do most of the Buddha and Bodhisattva figures in Buddhist paintings have smiles? The smiles were represented to show Buddha and Bodhisattva's kindness and their merciful feelings towards man's world - their smiles are mostly bright, clean and serene with strong inspiration.

Painting is also restricted by materials. Tools, materials and scientific and technical levels have an impact on painters' skills. Western painting broke through these restrictions and became developed thanks to scientific and technical development and the colours in western paintings became more vivid thanks also to scientific and technical development. Chinese painters preferred another kind of exploration: they broke the recognised way in tools and materials and adopted a vertical way of thinking in their method of observation. They developed their original tools and materials to a peak and made the cooperation between brush, ink and paper become more harmonious by further processing on brush pen and rice paper and each tool and material exposed its quality to the utmost in this cooperation. A brush pen can be used to draw the light-ink strokes of clouds, mist and remote overlapping mountains as well as fine, long silk. It can be used to depict clearly the thin, vibrating wings of a cicada, as well as vigorous sharp-cut cliffs. An ink colour can represent the dryness and withered scenes in autumn and winter, as well as moisture in spring and summer. A piece of paper can try its best to show the moving

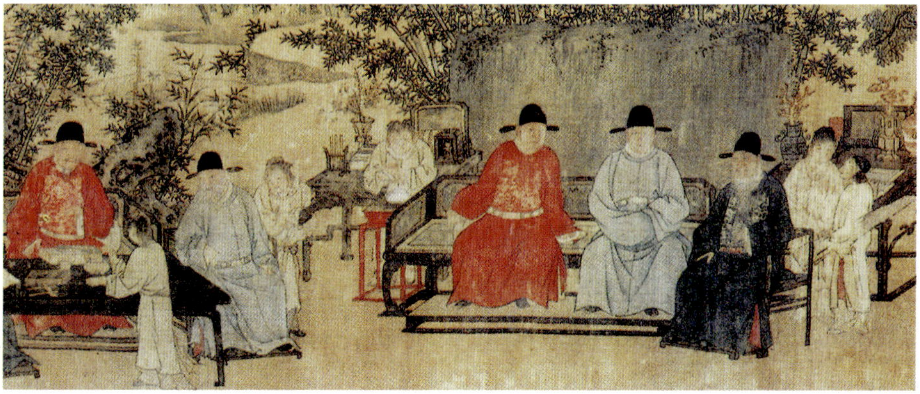

Xing Yuan Ya Ji Tu (Picture of Apricot Garden) (Part): By Xie Huan in the Ming Dynasty (1368-1644), scroll, Ink and color on silk 37 x 401cm, Preserved in the Zhenjiang Museum.

This painting features fine technique of drawing, thick color and orderly arrangement, showing the painter's better accomplishments.

state of the brush and can also distinguish the layers of ink subtly.

Painting was also restricted by another artificial element. There were many Looking for an opening in restrictions is the representation of Chinese people's intelligence. taboos in ancient China and violation of some of these taboos would result in the loss of lives. For example, the names of emperors, superior teachers and seniors and family eldership could not be mentioned directly and in daily life the emperors' names had to be changed; some colours, used exclusively by royal families, could not be used at random by common people; during some dynasties the former dynasty and relevant subjects could not be mentioned; and in some dynasties people had to be careful when creating literary works and paintings and if others drew the wrong conclusions by false analogy, they had to be punished. Under such preconditions painters would not, of course, select themes to paint at random.

The Chinese people are accustomed to and good at making restrictions.

The farming culture made Chinese people grow accustomed to restrictions by nature and the weather and people found out the rules of nature and the weather, guided their actions according to the rules and created freedom to the best of their abilities in dependency and harmony. Such a natural and happy relationship is known as the "harmony between man and nature."

Chinese people carried the relationship between man and nature into social relations and their national culture. The ethical relationship between monarch and officials and between seniors and juniors was management and obedience. In the national culture there is the theory that "no regulations, no square and round." Chinese people thought that regulations must be stipulated on creation and that creation against the regulations was not advisable; and a good creation must be

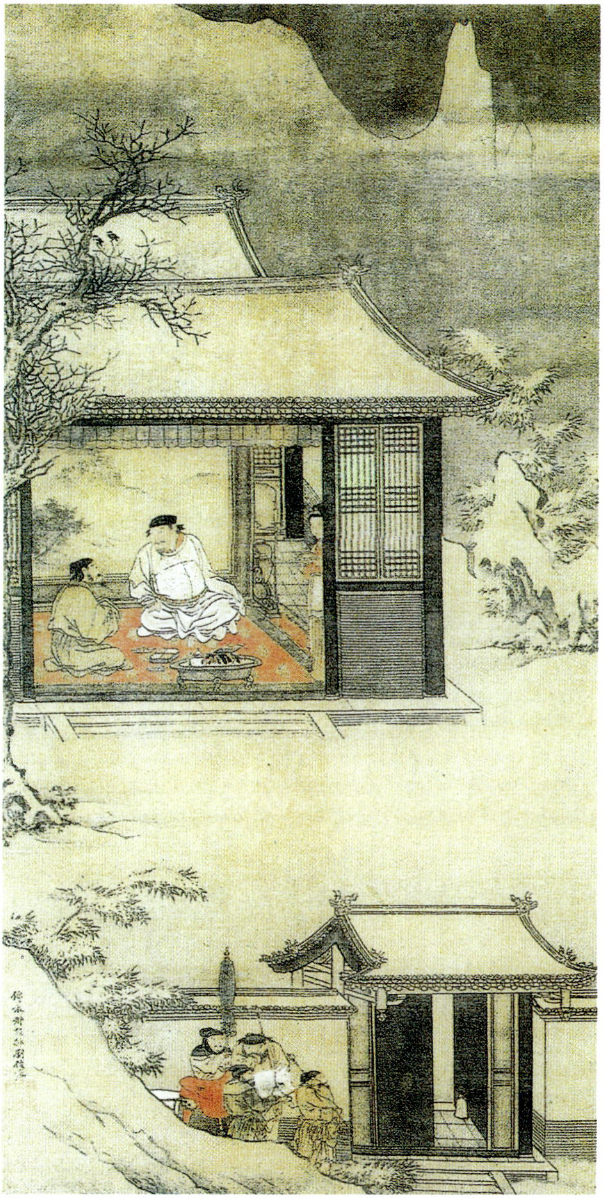

Xue Ye Fang Pu Tu (Picture of Visiting Pu in a Snowy Night): By Liu Jun of the Ming Dynasty (1368-1644), Ink and color on silk.

It is a successful painting depicting a story with clearly primary and secondary composition, prominent subject, vividly portrayed figures, and elegant and statedly tone.

according to the regulations and surprising at the same time. So in the minds of Chinese people creation without regulations lacked difficulty and challenge. They would not break the original natural restrictions and even created some artificial restrictions. Chinese painting is the visual representative of what was sought through the gaps in restrictions.

There were many restrictions which governed Chinese painting: simple tools and materials, simple colours, simple themes, restrictions by various ideologies and restrictions by various painting rules. Chinese painting and the artists' free will was bound by these tools, materials, colours, themes, social criteria and national thoughts. While seeking changes and freshness painters did not try to change these restrictions in order to realize the challenges facing them. The creation of a great accomplishment in conforming to these restrictions was to create ego in restrictions.

Chapter III: Express in a Flat Way and Place Feelings on the Landscape

——A Comparison of the Tendency in Themes between Chinese and Western Paintings

In both Chinese and western paintings people give priority to themes. There is an intersection between Chinese and western painting themes with the existence of differences at the same time. Different themes show the different cultural psychologies between the West and China: western people have direct and bold thoughts and deeds while Chinese people have indirect and suggestive thoughts and deeds.

DIFFERENT EXPRESSIVE WAYS ON SAME THEMES

Both Chinese and western paintings involve religious themes, fables and representations of figures, scenes and customs but they have different methods of representation.

Take religion as an example. Religious paintings in early times in the west were represented by mural paintings. After the start of oil painting independent paintings on easels became the major form of representation. In western paintings with

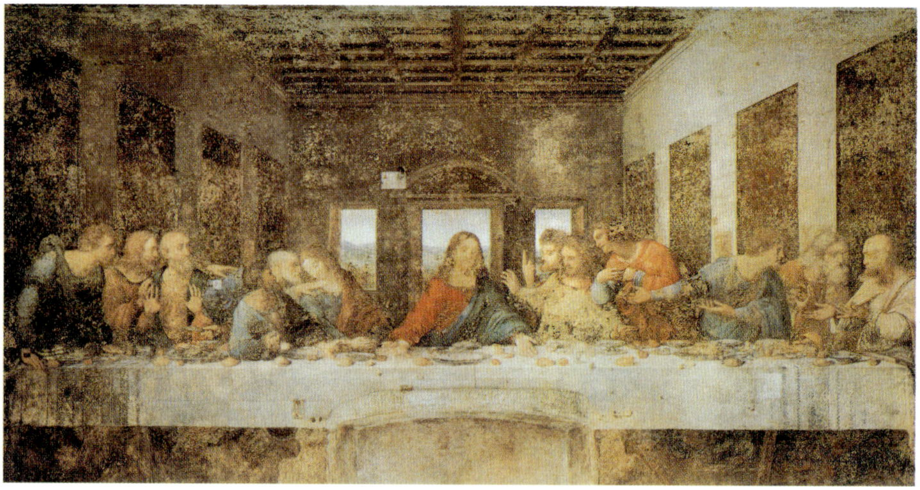

The Last Supper: 1495-1498, mural painting 420 x 910cm, by Leonardo da Vinci of Italy.

It represents the scene of The Last Supper from the final days of Jesus as narrated in the Gospel of John 13:21, when Jesus announces that one of his Twelve apostles would betray him. The figures in the painting line in a horizontal direction in different poses and with expressions, setting off the dignity and stillness of Jesus. This painting hightlights Jesus with the architectual perspective. Although paying tribute to Jesus, the painter adds dramatic scenario to the painting.

religious themes there are few face-figure pictures especially for worshiping and most of them have strong male emotions with plots. For example, *The Last Supper* by Leonardo da Vinci depicted a Christian story telling that Jesus knew he was betrayed by his disciple Judas and he wanted to expose the betrayer in public at the supper with all his disciples. The moment painted in the picture is about the chaos among Jesus' disciples when Jesus said "one of you has betrayed me." The expression and motion of each disciple in the picture tally with his personality. As to the psychology and emotions of the disciples depicted by the painter, similar models could be found in real life. It is said the image used for the betrayer is a dean of that time who embezzled money from clerics. Western religious paintings often sing in praises.

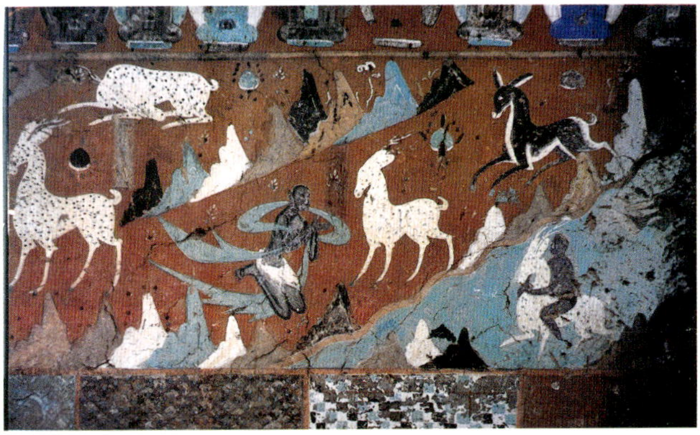

Lu Wang Ben Sheng (Part): Northern Wei Dynasty (386-534), Dunhuang No.257 Cave, Fresco

Fresco depicts a story. Before being Buddha, Sakyamuni changed himself into a nine-colored deer to save a drowning person. The one who was saved is greedy for money and betrays the nine-colored deer. At last he has skin ulcers on his body. Chinese early religious fresco had the functions of publicizing doctrines.

Chinese religious paintings principally display two functions, propagating doctrines and worship. Most of these paintings were done by folk painters and came in the form of mural paintings. In early times religious paintings involved the telling of Buddhist fables and parables and in later times most of these paintings were single figures just for worship. Some of them even have suppliers names painted on one side or at the bottom showing the utilitarian psychology in folk mentality. During the history of China many literary people converted to religion and many monks were painting masters but few of the religious paintings in China were painted by literary people. This strange circumstance was related to the Chinese literati's attitudes to religions, which were different from those of common people. Most common people practiced their religion with some prayers, hoping Buddha would protect them, while literary people preferred studying to worshipping and their expectations of themselves were higher than those of the gods. By studying Buddhist sutras they understood completely and kept an open mind on their lives and had stricter requirements on their own spirituality and life. So, literary people rarely painted Buddha figures for worship. They only blended their understanding and comprehension of studying Buddhist sutras into their paintings, making their paintings lofty and elegant.

NARRATIVE AND LANDSCAPE PAINTINGS

There are many differences in painting contents between Chinese and western paintings.

Western painters have a strong consciousness of participating in current political affairs and like to represent significant historical events. There are many painting themes related to significant historical events in the west. *The Massacre at Chios* by Eugene Delacroix drew its theme from the Grecian War of Independence. Greece had been dominated by Turkey for long time. In 1821 the Greek people rose up to resist their domination and declared

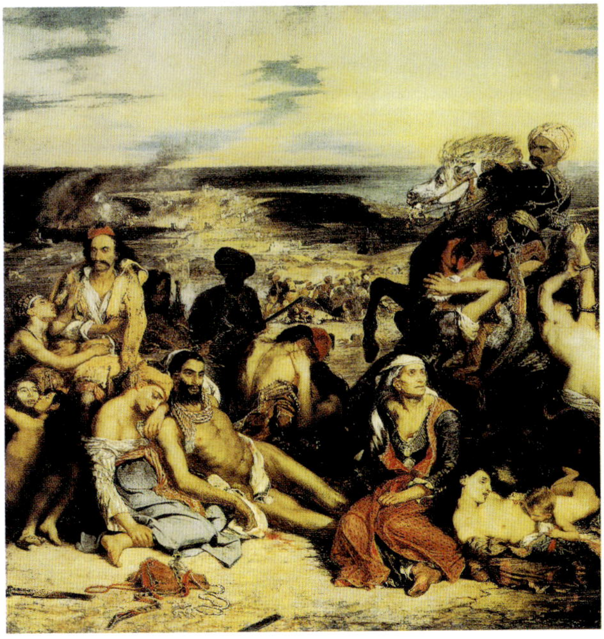

The Massacre at Chios: by Eugene Delacroix of France, 1824, oil on canvas 417 x 354cm, Preserved in the Louvre, Paris.

Delacroix's painting of the Massacre at Chios (also called Massacre at Scio, French: Sc è nes des massacres de Scio), shows sick, dying Greek civilians about to be slaughtered by the Turks.

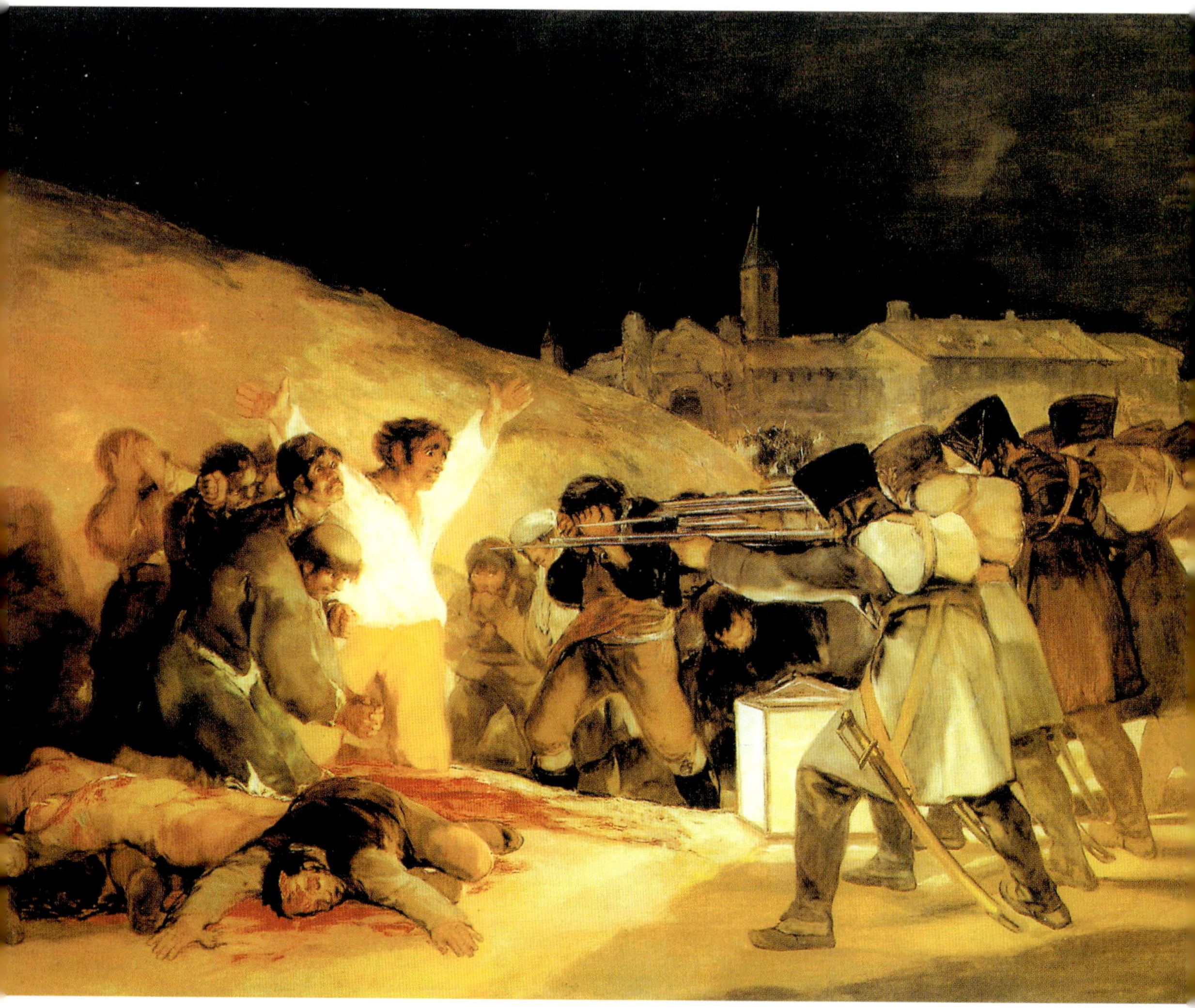

The Third of May 1808: The Execution of the Defenders of Madrid: 1814, Oil on canvas, Goya of Spain, Preserved in the Museo Del Prado Madrid.

It is a large-sized historical painting drawing its theme from the painter's eyewitness experience of the uprising. In 1808 Napoleon wanted to invade Spain and the cowardly Carlos Court submitted to him but the Spanish people did not want to live in colonization and rose in resistance.

independence. Their Turkish rulers launched a crucial suppression on Greece in the following year and more than 20,000 people were slaughtered on Chios. Many

European countries showed sympathy to and supported the Movement of Independence in Greece. They aided the movement and some of them directly participated in it. Eugene Delacroix represented sorrowfully and angrily the bloody and horrible slaughter and condemned the perpetrators brutality and inhumanity.

The Third of May 1808: The Execution of the Defenders of Madrid by Goya is a large-sized historical painting drawing its theme from the painter's eyewitness experience of the uprising. In 1808 Napoleon wanted to invade Spain and the cowardly Carlos Court submitted to him but the Spanish people did not want to live in colonization and rose in resistance. On May 2, 1808 the farmers in the suburbs of Madrid rose up but they were suppressed by the French army the following day. Goya expressed his anger and tragic feelings by depicting clearly the expressions on the faces of those who were killed.

Other famous paintings representing historical events include *The Surrender of Breda* by Diego Velazquez, *The Death of Marat* and *The Coronation of Napoleon* by David and *Bonaparte Visiting the Plague-Victims of Jaffa* by Gros and *Liberty Leading the People* by Eugene Delacroix. In these paintings painters used their brushes to record historical events and express their political views. China covers a large area and has a long history. Many significant historical events have occurred from ancient times to today, as well as countless changes of dynasties, social and scientific development, wars and reforms. When we look back into the history of painting in China there are almost no paintings related to significant historical events before the 20th century. Didn't Chinese painters care about politics? Yes, they did. Didn't Chinese painters love their country? Yes, they did. In fact, the Chinese literati painters were a group of people who especially worried about the country and its people and "every common man has his obligation for the improvement of the country" was always the belief held by them. In their hearts the rising and declining of the country was closely related to every one who had the obligation for the improvement of the country and should try his best to safeguard and construct the country. Few of the traditional literati paintings in China involve historical themes because, first of all, in history different arts in China shouldered different jobs and literature and other crafts (such as pottery, porcelain, building decorations and fine folk arts) took charge of the duty of recording and representing history. Secondly Chinese literary people thought it was wrong to resort to arms for solving issues and they always hoped to influence rulers by philosophical thoughts and ideals and thus reach the perfect social state by peaceful means. So they rarely dabbled in historical themes inclining to outside forces and only expressed their political tendencies and ideals through other themes.

In the National Palace Museum in Beijing there is a painting entitled Spring Outgoing by Zhan Ziqian, a famous painter of the Sui Dynasty (581-618). Among the older paintings in existence it is the oldest one showing a landscape as a theme. The figures in the painting are embroidered. Maybe someone before Zhan Ziqian produced similar works but his is the only example left. It is the earliest complete landscape painting among the extant paintings so it can be thought of as the pioneer and foundation for later Chinese landscape paintings.

Landscape and scene-and-plant paintings served to express the Chinese literati painters' political positions and expressed their personal emotions. Chinese literati painters enjoyed landscapes and they thought there was no profane flavour in landscapes and that it could cultivate higher qualities for people. In the Yuan (1271-1368) and Qing (1644-1911) dynasties there appeared many famous landscape painters whose painting styles were fresh, lofty, showing reclusive pride or vigorous

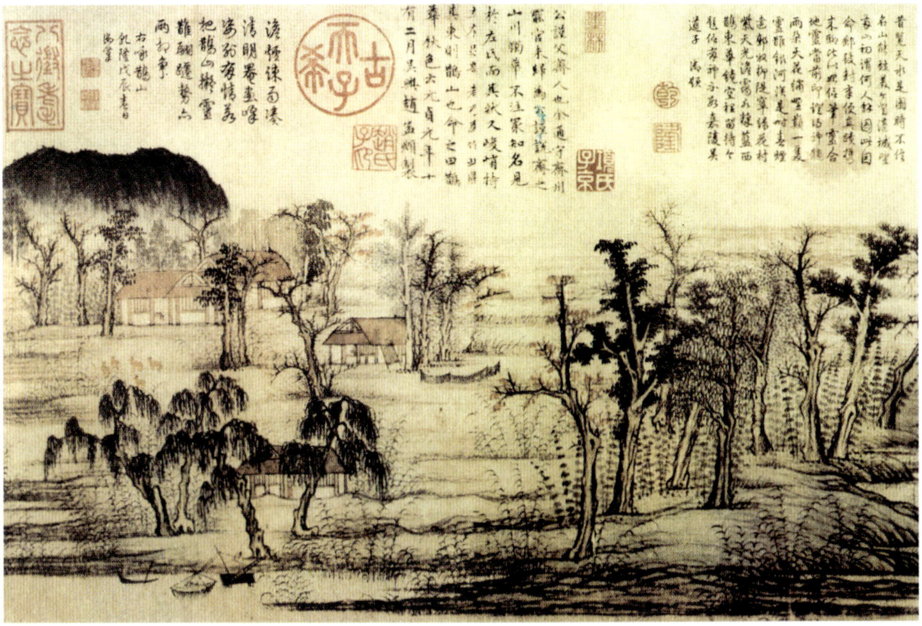

Scroll of *Autumn Colours on the Que and Hua*: by Zhao Mengfu, Ink and color on paper 28.4 x 93.2cm, Preserved in the National Palace Museum in Taipei

and full of anger and cynicism at society. These were the ways adopted by Chinese literati to express their dissatisfaction on current politics. For example, in the Yuan Dynasty after an ethnic minority united China they adopted the policies of national discrimination and class oppression. The feudalist scholars of the Han Nationality could not find their way into governments under such circumstance and felt extraordinarily bitter so most of them held the opinion that "serve the government if there is a way and be a recluse if there is no way," and looked for spiritual comfort from natural landscape painting. This was also shown in their literary creations. The following are examples of a "simple, leisurely, tranquil and watery" artistic concept; the *Autumn Colours on the Que and Hua* with "ink-spotted grasses and the reclusion, loftiness and elegance shown by surrounding greenery" by Zhao

Mengfu, the *Stone Cliff at the Pond of Heaven* with "overlapping green mountains with grand shrubs and forests" by Huang Gongwang and the *Picture of Watching the Mountain on the Opposite Bank of the River* with "a rainy day becomes sunny with the spring wind on the river and the setting sun is shining through the spring trees on the opposite river bank" by Ni Yunlin.

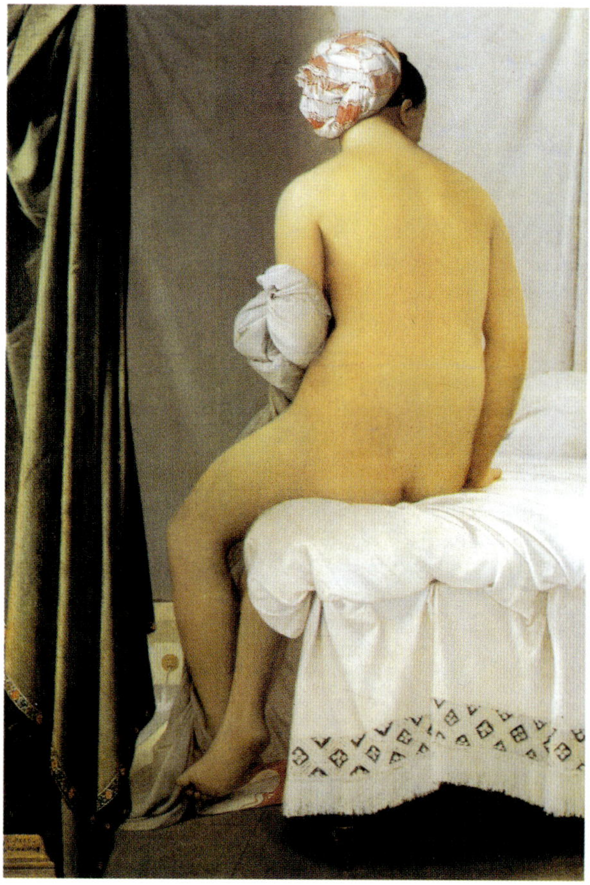

The Bather of Valpincon: 1808, oil on canvas 146 × 97.5cm, by Jean-Auguste-Dominique Ingres of France, Preserved in the Louvre, Paris.

Paying a tribute to the life through the human body is a major theme of the western paintings. This painting displays the harmon between body, lines and color.

Four plants, the plum blossom, the orchid, bamboo and the chrysanthemum are important themes in Chinese paintings. Chinese literati liked them and gave them different qualities to express feelings. In the eyes of the Chinese literati, the plum blossom is the symbol of self-independence, firmness and not going with the flow compared to their patriotic beliefs; the orchid is pretty and tall and it is different from other flowers. It has a faint fragrance and is not vulgar and it is a symbol of elegance; bamboo is hollow symbolizing modesty and the straight trunk is the symbol of maintaining integrity and not currying favour with influential officials; the chrysanthemum gets victory not due to its brilliant colour but because it blooms in autumn when other flowers fade and it can retain its fragrance long after withering and it is the symbol of uniqueness. With these subjective definitions, plum blossom, orchid, bamboo and chrysanthemum are called the "four men of integrity" by Chinese literati and became the hot objects in paintings. For example, Zheng Banqiao during the Qing Dynasty was famous for his orchid and bamboo paintings and his poems and paintings on bamboo are all portraits of his upright and unyielding quality. In the west there is no such cultural custom. Western people like to express their feelings and thoughts directly so there was no painting with special themes like these four kinds of plants.

Painting people is an important theme in western art. Western people attach importance to their own image and think the human body has a special beauty. A male body has the beauty of strength and fortitude and a female body has the beauty of charm and meekness, so many famous paintings represent the beauty of the human form. This is much different in Chinese customs. Chinese people do not think that direct exposure of the human body is beautiful but they like to enjoy indirect and implicated beauty. Therefore before the 20th century there were almost no Chinese literati paintings depicting the human body. When representing bodily beauty they have the aid of dresses and adornments.

Different themes show the different cultural psychologies between the West and China: western people have direct and bold thoughts and deeds while Chinese people have indirect and suggestive thoughts and deeds.

Chapter IV: Colours and Inks

——A Comparison of Colour Concepts and Usage between Chinese and Western Paintings

One of the main differences between Chinese and western paintings exists in inks and colours. Colours are the basis for western oil paintings while inks are the basis for Chinese paintings. Black is the only colour of ink used throughout the painting apart from the little red stamp of the seal. It is so inexplicable that no colours whatsoever are used to depict the fields, the green mountains, the rivers, the blue sky, loess, red flowers and green trees.

COLOURS AND INKS IN LANDSCAPES

The issue related to colours and inks is well represented in landscape paintings. Western landscape paintings are mostly landscape sketches and are comparatively true records of the scenery facing the painters in nature. When depicting nature, painters are shocked by the beauty of the natural scenery and find the colours of the environment are changing due to changes in light. The sun is giving out light at all times but because of the difference in weather conditions and the time of day the intensity of the light is constantly

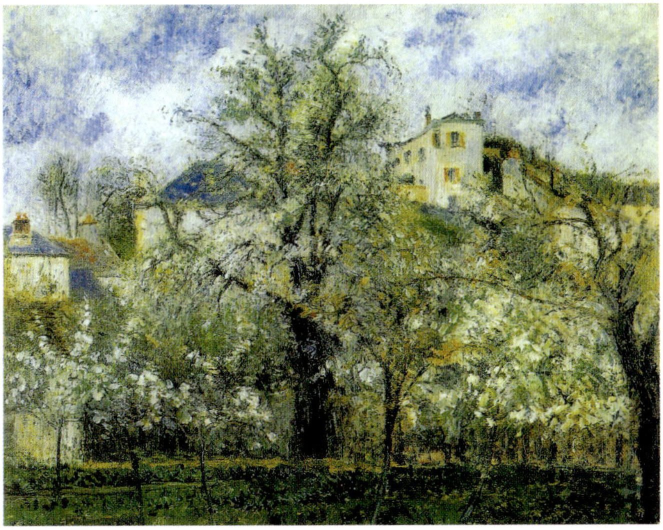

Kitchen Garden with Trees in Flower: By Camille Pissarro of France, 1877, oil on canvas 65.5 x 81cm, Preserved in the Mus é e d'Orsay, Paris.

Pissarro has always sought to vibrant color effect formed by sunshine and air. Known as the " Father of Impressionism", Pissarro painted rural and urban French life, particularly landscapes in and around Pontoise, as well as scenes from Montmartre. His mature work displays an empathy for peasants and laborers, and sometimes evidences his radical political leanings.

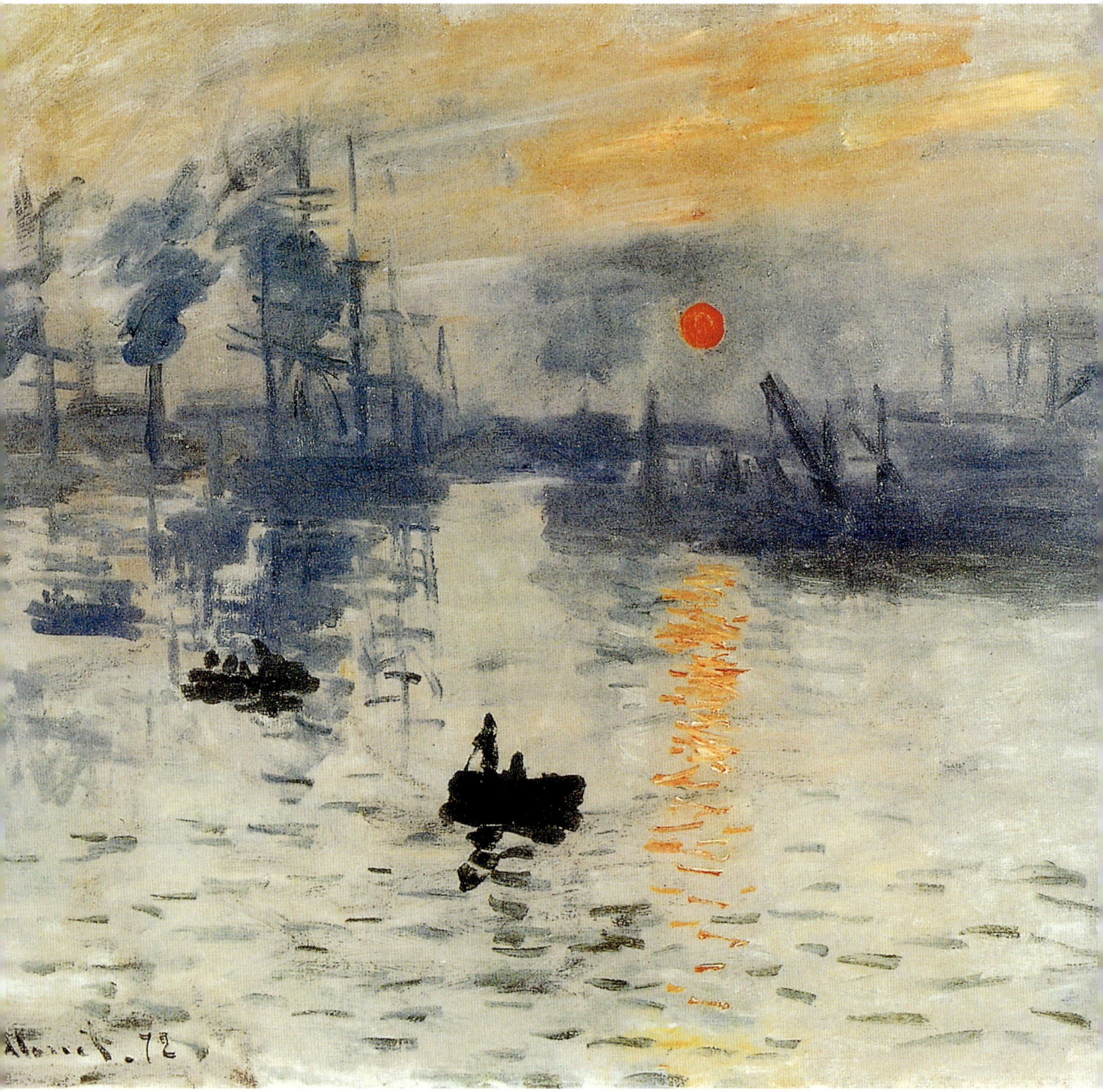

Impression, Sunrise, 1873, Oil on canvas 48 x 63cm, by Monet of France, Preserved in the Musee Marmottan-Monet, Paris.

Monet's painting marks the beginning of Impressionism's study on the relations between light and shadow's changes and color. This subject is the harbour of Le Havre in France, using very loose brush strokes that suggest rather than delineate it. For the Salon Academism artist, it is artistic rebel.

changing. Correspondingly the colours of nature change with the changes in sunlight. Painters are attracted by changes of sunlight and always want to seize a particular moment of sunlight in a picture. It is a challenge to the artists' ability to seize that moment and a competition in speed: the artists eyes must quickly seize the changes of sunlight and reproduce them. Some painters commit themselves to this challenge and study the relationship between changes in sunlight and shadow and the changes in colours and form their own painting style i.e. Impressionism. They push the lighter colours to a peak in their paintings and put other pure colours on the pictures to form tones by tactics or weaving strokes. On close sight the various colours in profusion look like a kaleidoscope and from a distance the different tones composed of the strokes constitute substance and bright and light shadows. Pure black is rarely seen in their paintings. In Impressionist paintings all the colour surfaces are composed of different spotted strokes. For example, what appears as a block of green surface is actually composed of yellow and blue spots along with purple and white spots of abundant visions and strong light shadow effect - colour palettes seem useless to them. Impressionism adopts the painting method of putting colours into full play but to other kinds of oil paintings colours are extremely important.

There are only a few colours in Chinese painting, black, white, red, blue, green and brown. In Chinese landscape paintings there are even fewer colours. Among the extant examples in existence only the "splendid and magnificent landscape" school created by Li Sixun during the Tang Dynasty (618-907) had comparatively strong colours. Even then the additional colours used by them only included blue, green and yellow and almost no other colours. In later water-ink landscape paintings there is only one colour of ink used. Black is the only colour of ink used throughout

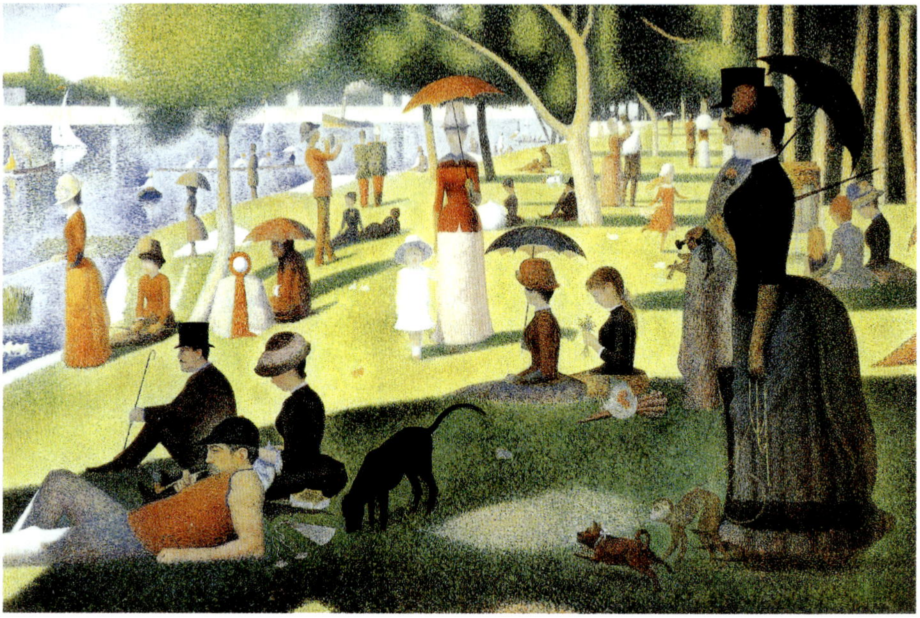

Sunday Afternoon on the Island of La Grande Jatte: by Georges Seurat of France, 1884-1886, oil on canvas 207 x 308cm, Preserved in the School of the Art Institute of Chicago.

Looking at Sunday Afternoon on the Island of La Grande Jatte by Georges Seurat, you will feel that a colour palette is unwanted, the points of the brushwork create a thoughtful exuberance of vision and colours and the transparency shown in the painting truly interprets the bright and beautiful sunlight.

the painting apart from the little red stamp of the seal. It is so inexplicable that no colours whatsoever are used to depict the fields, the green mountains, the rivers, the blue sky, loess, red flowers and green trees. push the lighter colours to a peak in their paintings and put other pure colours on the pictures to form tones by tactics or weaving strokes. On close sight the various colours in profusion look like a kaleidoscope and from a distance the different tones composed of the strokes constitute substance and bright and light shadows. Pure black is rarely seen in their paintings. In Impressionist paintings all the colour surfaces are composed of different spotted strokes. For example, what appears as a block of green surface is actually composed of yellow and blue spots along with purple and white spots of abundant visions and strong light shadow effect - colour palettes seem useless to them. Impressionism adopts the painting method of putting colours into full play but to other kinds of oil paintings colours are extremely important.

There are only a few colours in Chinese painting, black, white, red, blue, green and brown. In Chinese landscape paintings there are even fewer colours. Among the extant examples in existence only the "splendid and magnificent landscape" school created by Li Sixun during the Tang Dynasty (618-907) had comparatively strong colours. Even then the additional colours used by them only included blue, green and yellow and almost no other colours. In later water-ink landscape paintings there is only one colour of ink used. Black is the only colour of ink used throughout the painting apart from the little red stamp of the seal. It is so inexplicable that no colours whatsoever are used to depict the fields, the green mountains, the rivers, the blue sky, loess, red flowers and green trees.

Colour Taboos in Painting

There were colour taboos in all the past dynasties. The imperial colours could not be used at random in folk art and one such example is yellow.

Why was yellow a taboo colour in so many past dynasties? First, yellow is closest to the colour of gold. Among the Han nationality but before the Han Dynasty (206 BC - 220 AD) gold was the symbol of political power and man's power and gold was always used to produce sovereign seals, decorate chariots and waistband buckles. During the Han Dynasty, China exchanged silk for gold from Rome and other countries and by this commerce the national reserve of gold was increased very much. After the Han Dynasty, due to a sufficiency in gold and influences from foreign and ethnic minorities' ornaments, gold began to be used to produce female accessories. However, gold was always viewed as a metal for the nobility by Chinese people in all the later dynasties. So, yellow, the colour closest to gold, was also viewed as a noble colour. Secondly, yellow is close to the colour of a ripe field of grain. As Chinese people relied mainly on farming a field was the unit of dependence of living and generations of Chinese people had a feeling of being sentimentally attached to and depending on the field. Yellow is also close to the colour of grain in the fields and grain is the most fundamental need for human living and is as important as life. So, the rulers of all past dynasties in China kept a monopoly on yellow as the special colour of the ruling class and which has the same colour as gold and fields of grain. One example was that during the Qing Dynasty (1644-1911) only members of the royal family could dress in yellow.

As yellow is the symbol of power and is so bright that few other colours can suppress it, it is rarely used in Chinese art. Here we are talking about pure yellow as the use of gamboges which is between orange and brown or gold paint was adopted. Gold paint is as brilliant as yellow but not as showy and is distinguished with a vigour suppressing all others.

Five-colour Inks

The black, white, red, blue, green and brown inks used in Chinese paintings are almost all original colours in nature.

Black is the colour of night, Chinese people's hair and eyes and anything that is burned.

White is the colour of rice, ground wheat, clouds and the spray of rapid currents.

Red is the traditional Chinese colour of the sun, red flowers and blood.

Blue is the colour of the sky and the sea.

Green is the colour of leaves, grass and river water.

Brown is the colour of tree trunk and field.

Only these natural colours were used in Chinese painting implying that Chinese people attach importance to nature and its surroundings.

The sky holds a very high position in the hearts of Chinese people even higher than religion. Chinese fatalism is shown in such sayings as "submit to the will of heaven," "riches and honour depend on heaven," "man's plan is inferior to heaven's plan," and "man proposes, but Heaven disposes." Man's fate was not decided by his efforts but by "heaven". In Chinese fables the immortals lived in the unreachable heaven far away, an emperor who held supreme power was honoured as the son of heaven and intelligent people with accomplishments are called "talents of heaven." Chinese paintings especially depend on white symbolizing day and black symbolizing night.

In people's hearts day means light, activity, vitality and hope and night means peace, calm and depth.

In Chinese painting the way in which white is treated is very artful. White paint is sometimes used in Chinese painting especially in the traditional Chinese realistic paintings. Faint white is used along the inside edge of protruding lines to represent the turns on surfaces receiving a shine or raised surfaces but white paint is rarely used in traditional water and ink painting where the white is represented by the colour of the paper and this is called "leaving white."

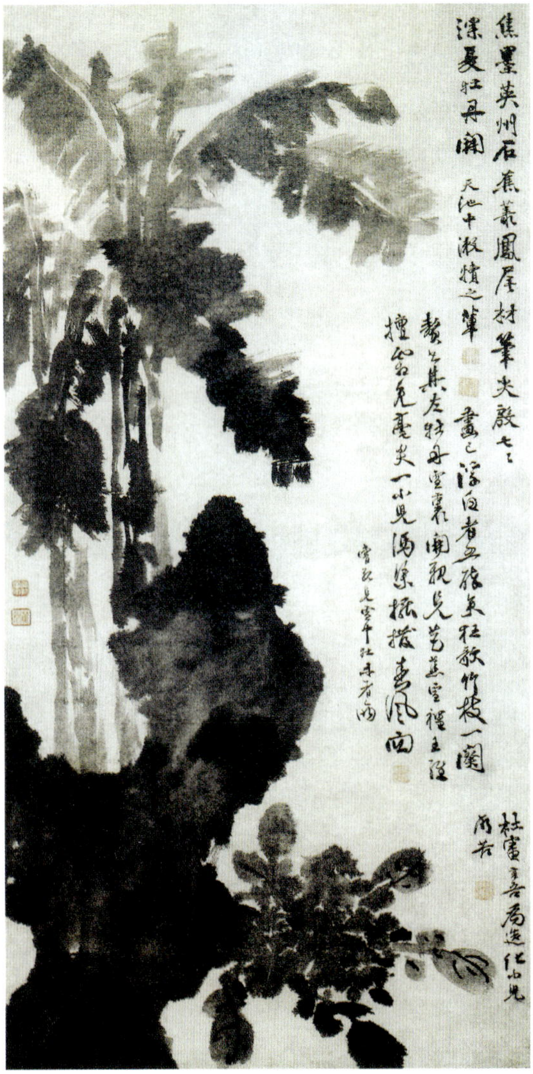

Mu Dan Jiao Shi Tu (Picture of Peony): By Xu Wei in the Ming Dynasty, Scroll, ink on paper 120.6 x 58.4cm, Preserved in the Shanghai Museum.

This painting is considered to be the most famous works of Xu Wei depicting the flowers with ink.

In western painting black is only viewed as one kind of colour and it is not used at random as it is thought to make pictures dirty, disorderly and stiff and to destroy the abundant and transparent colours. In particular, black is rarely used in watercolour painting. But to Chinese literati painting, especially the water and ink style of painting, colours are not the important factor. The colour of the ink and white are equally important but the real importance is attached to the feelings evoked in people. Black is the basic colour in Chinese calligraphy and art. In ancient times people burned willow branches to get a black pen and used it to draw drafts of murals and prepared Chinese ink is also black. The Chinese advocate steadiness. Children are cultivated to be steady. When praising a child receiving a good family education, you should praise him or her at first with, "you are steady, like an adult." Chinese people think only a person with a calm heart and a steady disposition is credible and can finish a task successfully. Chinese people, therefore, like the colour black as is gives that steady feeling.

Chinese painters think black is the steadiest colour and any picture without black is not steady and becomes floating. So no one can find a picture without black in traditional Chinese paintings. As Chinese painting depends so much on black, people have studied everything about black ink especially the layered effect. The changes between strong and light ink colours are brought about by various methods such as coating the paper, the mixing proportions between ink and water, amount and ways of dipping the brush into the ink and the ways of touching and moving the brush on paper. Then the changes in colour result in abundant aesthetic feelings. There is a saying in Chinese painting, "there are five kinds of ink colour (dry, wet, strong, light and burnt)."

Dry ink uses little water and is often used to paint light-ink strokes on mountains and stones to produce the feeling of vigour and void.

Wet ink uses a lot of water when it is mixed and applied to a drawing or used to draw points of leaves or moss in a rainy scene so that the picture has the feeling of humidity or used in splash-ink painting to represent the flavour of a water-ink painting with humidity.

Light ink is often used to draw remote objects or the bright surfaces of objects.

Strong black ink is often used to draw near objects or the dark surfaces of objects.

Burnt ink is blacker than strong ink and is often used to emphasise the blackest part of a picture by sketching, pointing or light-ink strokes.

Chapter V: Rich-colour Painting and Light Water-ink Painting

——Arison of Skills between Chinese and Western Paintings

The concentrated observation method and the depth representation by focus perspective in Europe made European paintings have a three-dimension space, while the loose observation method and the scattered-points spreading arrangement in China made Chinese paintings become comparatively plane. Painting is an art blending addition and subtraction. Such addition and subtraction relies on two aspects: the technical and the spiritual aspects. Chinese painting combines generalization and representation. The generalization in Chinese painting includes both the external generalization of techniques and the internal abstraction and generalization of the spirit.

Focus and Scattered-points Perspective

Listen to a choral performance of Chinese children followed by one by western children. If you listen carefully you will find that the chorus by the Chinese children differs greatly from that of the western children. In the chorus of the western children you will distinguish the voice of each one in the sound mixture and each voice is given out after turning round in his or her mouth. The chorus is stereo and the blending of many stereo voices seems like the gathering of many balloons - spaces are left in the blending, so the sound is penetrating and changeable in echoes with clear layers. The chorus of the Chinese children is silvery and clean, close to unison without much difference between each voice. Due to the numerous participants, many voices enlarge one tone and the increase in numbers of participants only results in increase in volume. Therefore, the chorus of the Chinese children has commonness and is on a single plane. It is a beauty of clearness and joy and is penetrating.

This principle also applies to painting. European painting is stereo while Chinese painting is on a plane. There are many reasons for this. The first reason for many people is that it is a result of perspective. The focus perspective is adopted in European painting with a strong feeling of space and a third dimension while a scattered-points perspective is adopted in Chinese painting everywhere so it is on the one plane. Visually this is clearly so.

The Holy Trinity is a religious mural created by Masaccio. For the first time he adopted space perspective in painting. The longitudinal division lines of the vault join finally to a point in the depth of the picture. Masaccio placed the major figures of the Holy Father and the Son in superposition and before the perspective focus and the Son with the focus of light is set off by the dark-coloured robe of the Father. Using such an arrangement and treatment people immediately pay attention to the focus of the picture, which is much more prominent and with clear layers.

In the mural *The Delivery of the Keys* by Pietro Perugino the figures are not placed in focus, but a method of contrast is adopted. He deepened the space by a focus perspective and spread the major figures in front of the space bringing the audience closer to the figures in the picture.

The Last Supper by Leonardo da Vinci and *The School of Athens* by Raphael carried forward the treatment in *The Holy Trinity* by Masaccio. Along the longitudinal perspective lines on up, down, left and right of the building in the picture the audiences' lines of sight are finally attracted to the major figures. Leonardo da Vinci and Raphael made some improvements on this style. They placed the focus on outdoor space far away creating the feeling of penetration with the deepened space. Solid figures are set off by a vacant space and the major figures are set off by a bright and simple background and the effects are stronger. In another master piece by Leonardo da Vinci, the *Mona Lisa*, the head of the figure was placed in a comparatively bright and naturally perspective environment, so the monotone background was broken and the major figure was prominent.

The Avenue at Middelhamis by Hobbema, *Barbizon Forest* by Rousseau and *Marshland* by Charles-Francois Daubigny are all oil landscapes. There are definite

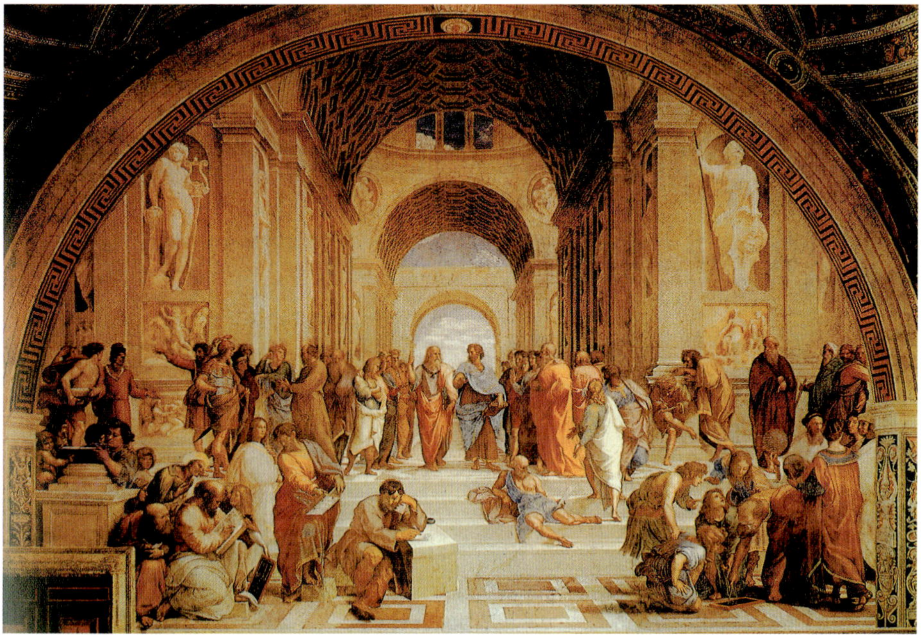

The School of Athens: By Raphael of Italy, 1501-1511, Fresco 620 x 280cm, Preserved in the Vatican City Museum.

It represents numerous figures in different poses and their different characters, which shows the prominent talents of Raphael when aged 27. The composition of this picture shows that Raphael is accomplished in the focus perspective.

perspective lines on the pictures and it is easy to find the foci of the pictures. Using such a method the space has a strong longitudinal depth and a prominent third dimension.

In many famous Chinese paintings concerning landscape or social customs, such as the *Scroll of the Fishing Ship on the Autumn River* by Xu Daoning, the *Scroll of the Snow in a Fishing Village* by Wang Shen, the *Scroll of a Thousand-mile Landscape* by Wang Ximeng and *Qingming Festival by the Riverside* by Zhang Zeduan from the Song Dynasty (960-1279) plus the *Scroll of Chibi* by Wu Yuanzhi from the Jin Dynasty (1115-1234) and the *Scroll of Autumn Colours on the Que and*

Hua by Zhang Mengfu, the *Scroll of Habitation in Fuchunshan Mountain* by Huang Gongwang and the *Scroll of a Sunny Day after Autumn Rain in a Fishing Village* by Ni Zan fromthe Yuan Dynasty (1271 -1368), there was no treatment of perspective focus like in European oil paintings. The visual center of these paintings is not a focus and the visual points are broad horizontally or vertically. Notwithstanding the difference between remote mountains and near rivers, the scattered visual points weaken the depth of space. As a conclusion when compared to the three-dimensional European oil paintings, Chinese paintings look like they are on a plane.

Let's think about the course of studying painting. When studying European painting you should study the sketching before the colours. Even if the courses of

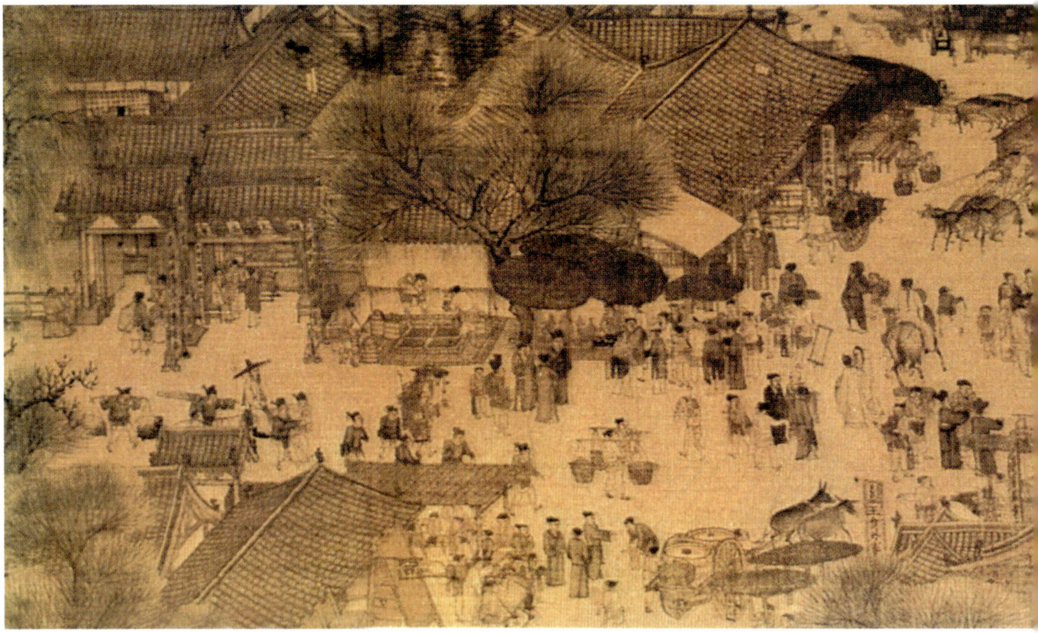

Qingming Festival by the Riverside: by Zhang Zeduan of the Song Dynasty, Ink and color on silk 24.8 x 528 cm, Preserved in the Palace Museum in Beijing.
Chinese paintings show the spreading scattered-points perspectives.

sketching and colours are arranged for the same time in a school the teachers of colour courses will emphasize the importance of space and arrangement besides teaching the rules of colour. It can be said that painting colours is a course of painting sketches by colours. So, sketching is the basis of Eu-

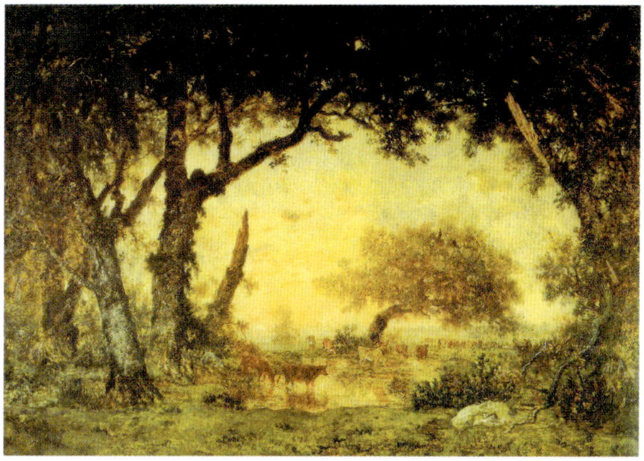

Barbizon Forest: 1848-1849, oil on canvas 142 × 197.5cm, by Theodore Rousseau of France, Preserved in the Louvre, Paris.

Theodore Rousseau is a French landscape painter, one of the founders of the Barbizon School. This paintins is his masterpiece.

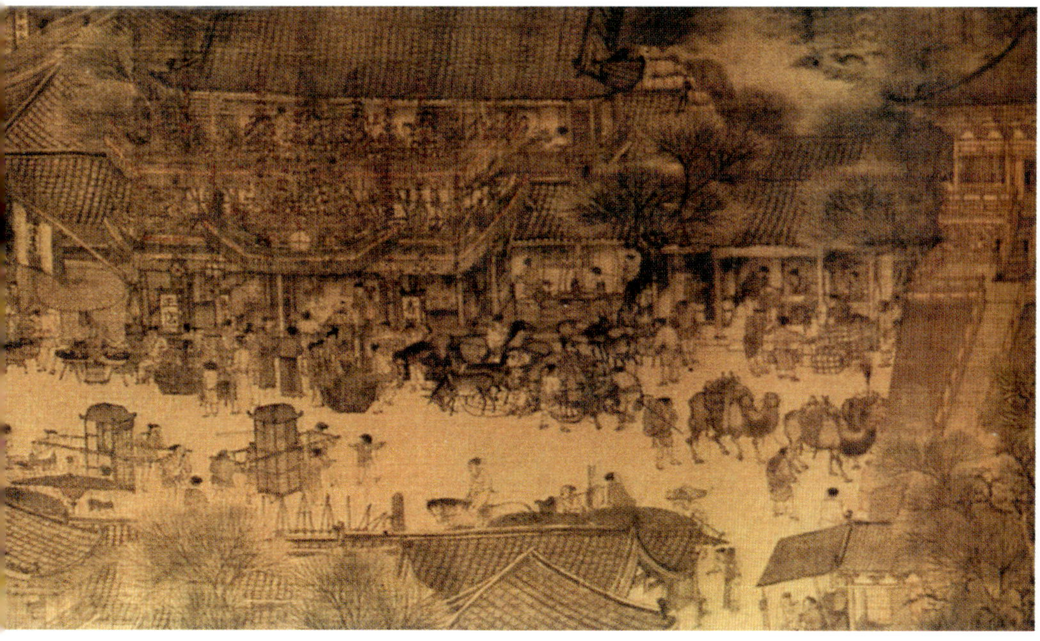

ropean painting. Why? Because sketching is not only copying objects monochromatically according to its literal meaning but also it is a method of training on observing and representing objects in nature. Teachers will often say, "close one eye, stretch out your pen and measure the proportion of objects with one eye". You will find it is difficult to measure an object exactly by stretching out the pen and looking with both eyes open but once one eye is closed you can measure more exactly. Therefore, painting the object on paper according to the proportion measured by the pen and the space relationship is confirmed approximately. Then some strong or light colours are applied according to the light and the shadow, so that the third dimension is represented on the paper. To sketch is to create a three-dimensional space on a plane.

But focus and scattered-points perspectives are only visual factors and the profound reasons rely on the differences in lifestyle and culture between China and the West.

Lifestyle influences cultural modes. After people obtain a reaction from a same action over a long period of time such an action would be remembered as a conditioned hereditary reflex and become an instinct after being passed down for several generations. The focus-perspective observation way in Europe might be

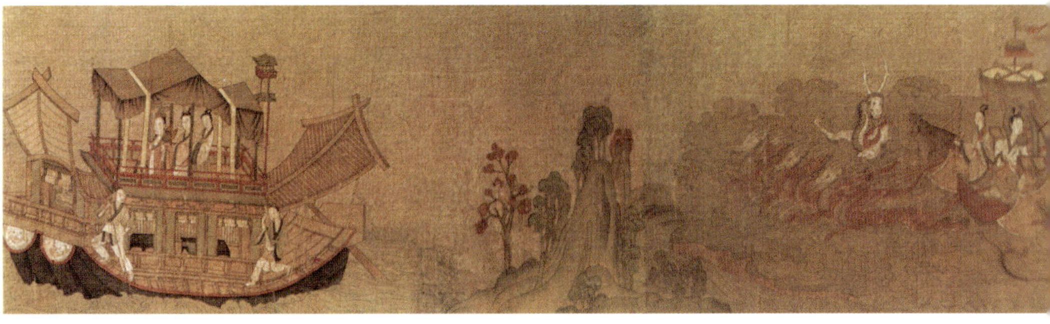

Luoshen Fu Tu (The Nymph of the Luo River): by Gu Kaizhi in the Eastern Jin Dynasty, Ink and color on silk, 27.1 x 572.8 cm, Preserved in the Palace Museum in Beijing

from such hereditary experience. Early European ancestors lived by hunting animals and they could only succeed in hunting animals if they focused on their prey completely. In the course of hunting they discovered the advantages in positioning by single-eye observation which became the norm in their memory. Hunting made European people good at single-eye observation and cultivated their concentration on things. In order to have such hunting concentration the key point of vision must be unidirectional and deep. Before the Middle Ages European painting was also on a plane but this could only be explained by the fact that people at that time did not have enough variety of methods or the ability to paint or to represent really the visual effects they wanted.

European science and technology developed in a deep way and people often researched on structural units of matters by dissection and partition. What are the minimum structural units? How do they compose the shape and features of matter? They achieved accomplishments in each field along with the questions. Depending on their longitudinal visual action and their thinking, as well as their profound analysis, they studied the principle of focus perspective and adopted it in painting and it was not strange for them to create the three-dimensional space in painting.

In European painting, people use only one eye to observe while in Chinese

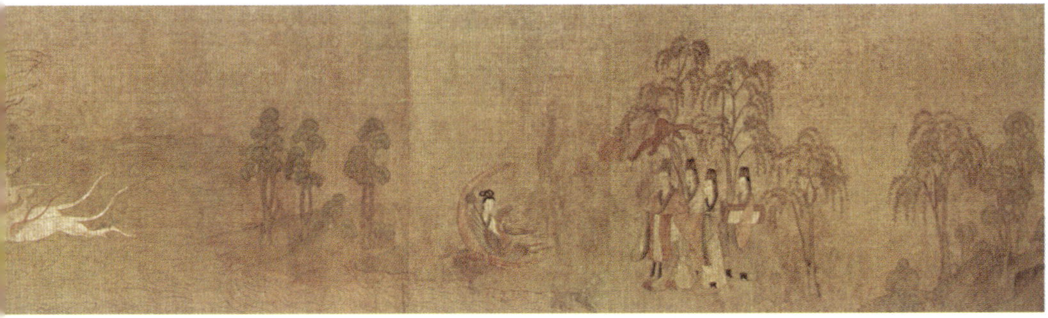

painting people use their two eyes to observe. Some people may ask did our Chinese ancestors not hunt animals? Our Chinese ancestors once depended on fishing and hunting but later they changed their main ways of making a living to agricultural and farming and hunting became only a minor way to improve life. Hunting became much more insignificant especially after learning how to domesticate animals.

The farming life of our Chinese ancestors resulted in a scattered-points vision. On a broad plain without anything blocking the eyesight you will see boundless fields and sky when looking straight ahead. When exhausted by tedious and repeated labouring face down and back to the sky, people would unconsciously pay attention to moving things while resting in an upright position. They would observe birds flying in the sky, frogs in the water, people walking on their way, butterflies in the air and swaying branches and leaves in the wind. Then people's vision became loose along with the movement. Compared to tedious labouring people liked the loose feeling. Because of this loose vision people got several sequential visual impressions, so Chinese people adopted the side-by-side arrangement when treating objects in painting. For example, horizontal side-by-side arrangement was adopted in the *Picture of the Emperors of Past Dynasties* by Yan Liben and *Han Xizai Yeyan Tu (the Night Revels of Han*

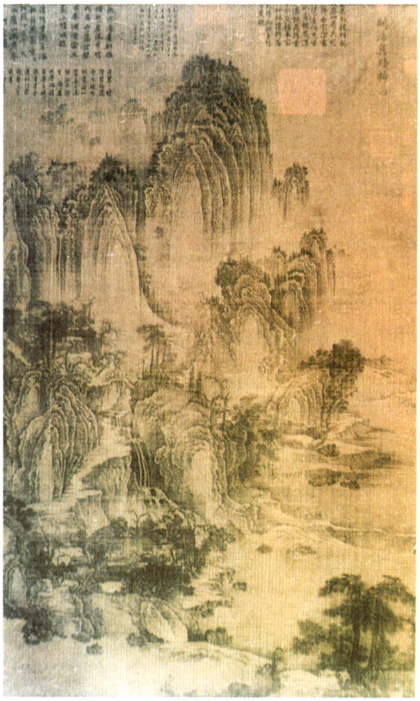

Scroll of Kuanglu: by Jing Hao in the Five Dynasties, Ink on silk 185.8 x 106.8 cm, Preserved in the National Palace Museum in Taipei

Xizai) by Gu Hongzhong and vertical side-by-side arrangement was adopted in the *Scroll of Kuanglu* by Jing Hao and the *Scroll of Travel in Guanshan Mountain* by Guan Tong. The composition is a side-by-side arrangement on a plane no matter whether it is horizontal or vertical, so the pictures give people the feeling of being on a plane. Notwithstanding the difference between remote and near objects in the *Scroll of Kuanglu* by Jing Hao and the *Scroll of Travel in Guanshan Mountain* by Guan Tong, the depth was weakened by the spreading side-by-side arrangement and they also give a feeling of being on a plane.

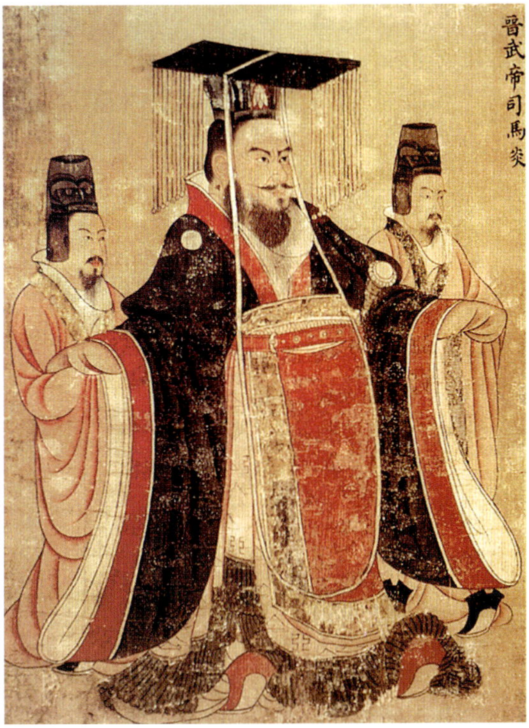

Picture of the Emperors of Past Dynasties: By Yan Liben in the Tang Dynasty, Ink and color on silk 51.3 x 531cm, Preserved in the Museum of Fine Arts, Boston, the US.

Emperors are the important and popular theme of Chinese ancient paintings. The Emperor in this painting is Sima Yan, Emperor Wudi of the Jin Dynasty, whose martial blood and bearing are depicted incisively and vividly.

The concentrated observation method and the depth representation by focus perspective in Europe made European paintings have a three-dimension space, while the loose observation method and the scattered-points spreading arrangement in China made Chinese paintings become comparatively plane.

SURFACE AND LINE

From sketches to colours western paintings have always attached importance to the exactness of shapes and expanding the depth of space. Painting on a plane became painting in three-dimensions and painters tried their best to represent all the visual realities in their painting. As to both sketching and colouring, painters rarely used single-lines to draw the outline of an object clearly, as drawing lines tended to create the feeling of a plane and destroyed the three-dimensional feeling. In European paintings even the most definite turning line will not be represented directly by a line. Sketches are represented by different arrangements or different densities of touching points and colours are represented by changes in colours. Concisely, European paintings make the most of the surface instead of the lines.

It is interesting that lines are indispensable for drafts of both sketches and colours to confirm the whole structure and the position and outline of each part. But these lines are so light that in the course of spreading tone in sketches or colouring the draft lines are covered and after finishing the painting, all the draft lines disappear and people can only see the surface, shape, light, shadow and colours.

It is completely contrary to Chinese painting which prefers representation by lines. Lines are indispensable in Chinese art from ancient to modern paintings.

Chinese people like to find the skeleton of objects. And the basic forms of skeleton are simple or complex lines, so Chinese people like lines. Chinese paint ers like to represent skeletons and the looks of objects by lines that are flexible and changeable. The shortest line can be a point, a straight line can be vigorous and firm, a curved line can be moving, changing and smooth and arranged or crossed lines can compose surfaces of various shapes and sizes. So, a variety of lines can be seen in traditional Chinese paintings.

During the Shang (16-11th centuries BC) and the Western Zhou (11th century - 771 BC) dynasties, metal crafts and jade carving were well developed and until the Warring States Period (475-221 BC), the crafts of metal carving and gold and silver inlay were very skilled. Jade carving, metal carving and gold and silver inlay all involved carving exact, smooth lines on hard materials, which exercised man's ability in using tools, material qualities and strength. The lines became more

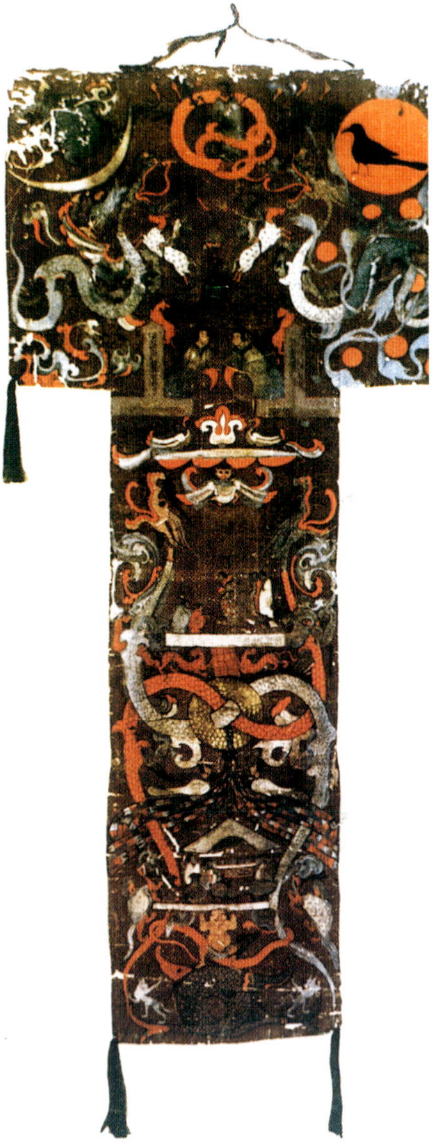

Mawangdui T-shaped Silk Painting: the Western Han Dynasty. 205 cm long and 92cm wide on the upper end and 47.7cm wide on the lower end, Unearthed from Mawangdui, Changsha, Hunan Province, Preserved in the Hunan Provincial, Museum

and more vigorous and smoother. Such hard material crafts as jade and metal are different from painting but there are profound mutual influences between them. Hard material crafts seek for smooth and light lines like painting touches and painting was influenced by the strength in hard material crafts - the lines in the paintings of the Warring States Period and Han Dynasties (206 BC - 220 AD) have the vigour and flexibility of coiled metal threads, such as the *Silk Painting of a Dragon Figure and a Phoenix*, the *Silk Painting of an Imperial Dragon Figure*, and the *Mawangdui T-shaped Silk Painting*. Another mural of the Eastern Han Dynasty (24-220 AD), *Picture on the Outgoing*, is more vivid in persuasion: the lines of the horse and carriage in the picture are extremely plump and the strength and flexibility possess distinctive time characters that are incom parable to prior dynasties.

During the Han Dynasty (206 BC - 220 AD), another style of simple, general and

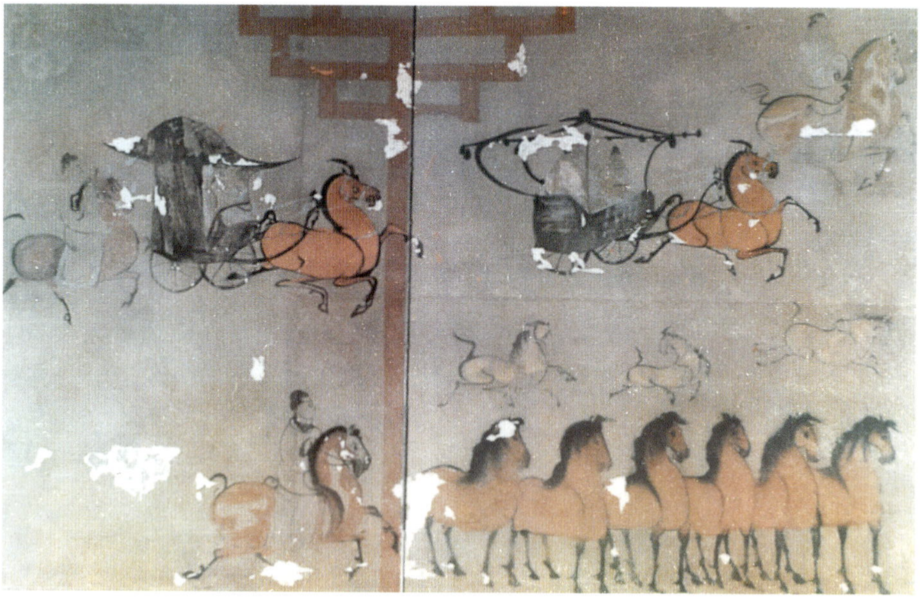

Picture on the Outgoing: the Eastern Han Dynasty. Unearthed from Helinger County, the Inner Mongolia Autonomous Region, fresco

vigorous lines appeared in painting. They lacked flexibility and tenacity and had more toughness, strength and firmness. They were the paintings in brick and stone carvings. During the Han Dynasty the craft of stone and brick carving was developed the same as or even better than pure painting. Stone carving is a kind of one-off subtraction craft that cannot be changed or patched up. At first when people adapted to the craft they naturally used silhouette-like shapes to represent the image because more detailed lines would bring in increased difficulties. With the progress in tools and technology detail lines and texture effects appeared in stone carving.

In the Wei and Jin dynasties (220-420 AD) importance was attached to carrying forward the smooth lines of the Han Dynasty (206 BC - 220 AD) and one line could connect two or more parts of an object. For example, in the Picture of Hunting with a Bow and Arrow in the coffin chamber of Wei and Jin in the Jiayuguan Pass, one line was used to paint the heads, necks, backs and tails of the running horses and deer and subtle turns were used to represent the connecting relationship between each part and uninterrupted lines were used to set off the fluent running shapes of the animals.

Smooth lines which looked endless were developed into continuity and consistency by Gu Kaizhi, such as the lines in the *Picture of Nu Shi Zhen (Admonition of Female Officials).*

Such continuous and consistent lines were inherited and carried forward by painters of later generations. Li Zhaodao of the Tang Dynasty (618-907 AD) even used such lines to paint stones and mountains (see the *Picture of the Emperor Ming Visiting Shu).* Later Wu Daozi added twists and turns in the smooth lines showing the beauty of the rise and fall and the moving wind smoothly, and created the famous "Wu's band seems like the wind."

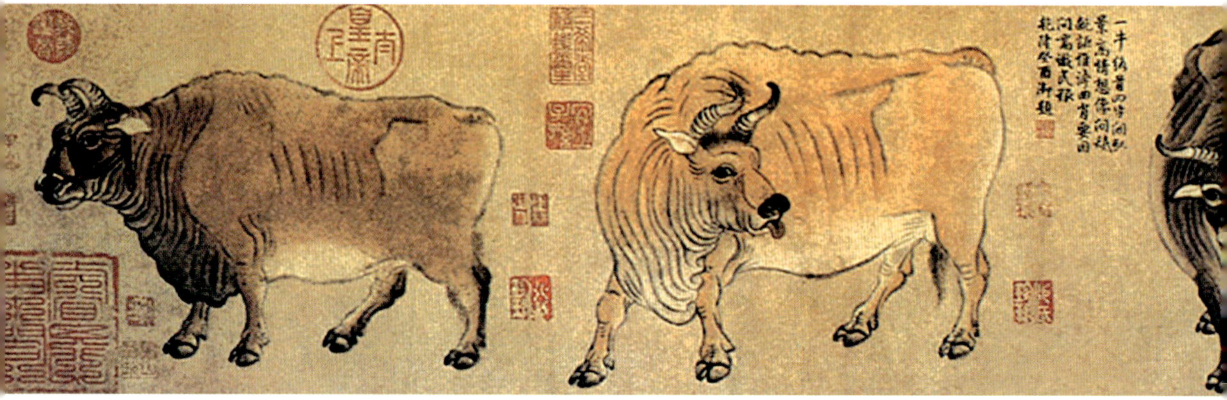

Picture of the Five Oxen: By Han Huang in the Tang Dynasty, Ink and color on silk 20.8 x 139.8 cm, Preserved in the Palace Museum in Beijing

In the *Picture of the Five Oxen* by Han Huang on the outline of the backs, lines of twists and turns were used to represent the bones of the oxen's backs, hard-turn corner lines were used to represent the rear hips and round-turning lines were used to represent the parts below the neck. The usage of different lines made shapes more concise and the picture more abundant.

In the *Zhao Ye Bai* by Han Gan mainly smooth and round-turning lines were used to represent the plump and vigorous muscles of the horse and hard-turn corner lines were used to represent the vigorous legs and hoofs of the horse.

From the Five Dynasties (907-960 AD) the continuous lines adopted before the Tang Dynasty (618-907 AD) changed. In the *Scroll of Figures in Liuli Hall* by Zhou Wenju, sectioned and overlapped lines were used to represent structures and changing short lines were used to represent the grains on the clothes showing the movement of brush pen on silk.

After the Song Dynasty (960-1279 AD) painters used continuous or short, smooth or paused, and soft or vigorous lines to show the variety and changeable

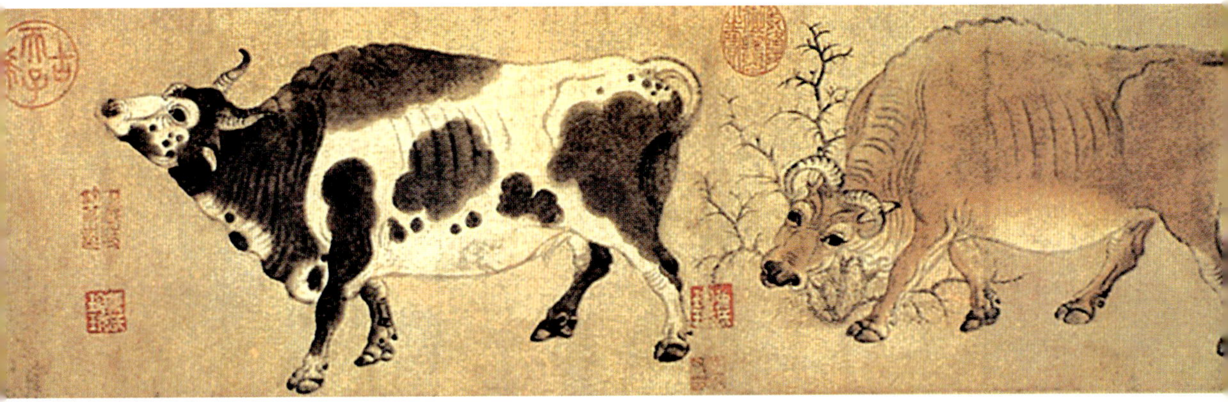

shapes of all objects. Some painters were more magic, they could use turned and continuous lines without any straight lines to show exactly vigorous, heavy mountains and stones, such as Guo Xi, Xiao Zhao and Li Gonglin.

Since ancient times China has created intelligent use by developement. People attached importance to

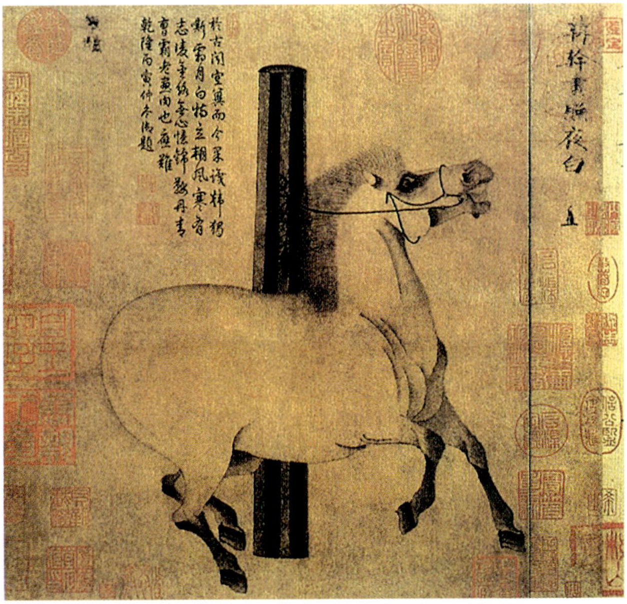

Zhao Ye Bai Tu Juan (Scroll of Zhao Ye Bai): By Han Gan, Ink and color on paper 30.8 x 33.5cm, Preserved in the Metropolitan Museum of Art, New York

"Zhao Ye Bai" is one of horses of Li Longji, Emperor Xuanzong of the Tang Dynasty. The painting depicts the horse raising its head and whinnying. Mainly smooth and round-turning lines were used to represent the plump and vigorous muscles of the horse and hard-turn corner lines were used to represent the vigorous legs and hoofs of the horse.

the features of tools, so it was with painting. After representing the abundant expressions of lines, skills of pen-points, to their utmost abilities Chinese literati painters started to study the expression power of the side-blade and surface of the pen and the sense of reality on the surface, which were mainly represented by various light-ink strokes and painting methods.

It should be said that Chinese painting also paid attention to changes of surfaces. For example, a painter should observe the changes in indented and protruding surfaces, facing or opposing light, thinness and thickness, tallness and shortness and edges and corners when painting stones. When showing the differences between surfaces facing and opposing the light of stones the ink is light and little on the surface facing light and it is strong and much on the surface opposing the light. After differentiating the surfaces facing or opposing the light, painters should show the

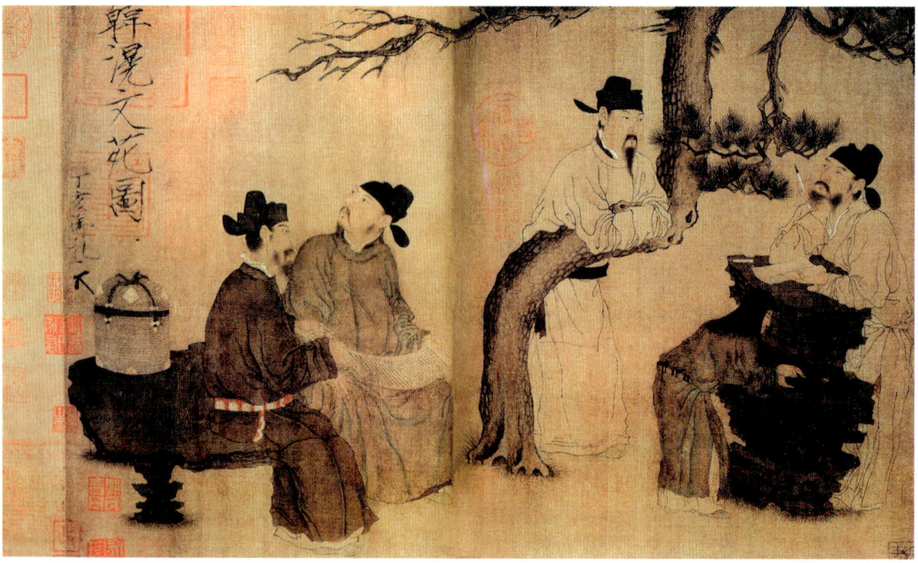

Liu Li Tang Ren Wu Tu Juan (Scroll of Figures in a Hall Inlayed with Colored Glaze): By Zhou Wenju in the Five Dynasties, Ink and color on silk 37 × 58.5cm, Preserved in the Palace Museum in Beijing.

differences between stones with different geological structures and materials in different regions. The painting method representing mountain stones, tree textures and a sense of reality is called “cun (light-ink strokes)”. To show the stone textures and sense of reality, various methods of cun can be used such as “putting on spots cun", "untying chain cun", "raindrop cun", "rolled cloud cun”, “ox hair cun”, “lotus leaves cun”, “broken band cun”, “iron end of arrow cun”, “big axe cleaving cun” and “small axe cleaving cun”. In “axe cleaving cun”, comparatively dry ink is used with the side blade of a brush pen that sweeps the paper with some force and speed and then the flat surfaces of the mountain stones look like they are being cleaved by an axe.

In the artful treatment on surfaces in Chinese painting there is another typical example, painting a shrimp head. Dip the point of the pen and the middle blade of the pen into the ink, use another clean pen and dip it into clean water, make the clean water drop on to the root of the pen with ink and then the ink and water are mixed gradually from the pen-point to the pen-root. Put such a pen exactly and definitely on the paper on its side blade and then raise it up and then the main part of a clear shrimp head comes into being on the paper. The front part is pointed and the back part is round. The pointed part is sharp and solid and the round part is transparent and glittering. One touch represents the reality. Such intelligent use was created during the long usage of brush pens.

Most of the surfaces in Chinese paintings are concise and close to the essence and painters try best to represent the shapes and sense of reality of surfaces by simple methods.

ADDITION AND SUBTRACTION

Painting is an art blending addition and subtraction. Such addition and subtraction relies on two aspects: the technical and the spiritual aspects.

European painting is an art with continuous addition, dual addition on technical and spiritual aspects. In the aspect of techniques, European paintings are composed of overlapped colours and in oil paintings especially, paints can be covered together. Usually the rule of applying colours is from light to deep colours but, if required, deep colours can be covered by light ones. For example, when painting high-light points, deep colours are covered by white. Every painting has its aim and meaning and when the objects or images are moving pictures, humanistic values are added into the objects. In this term, painting does spiritual addition as well as technical addition.

In Chinese paintings, colours are usually applied flat inside outlines drawn by ink lines and different colours are arranged side by side and rarely added together. So, in terms of colours, what Chinese painting does is arrangement and combination.

Chinese water and ink xieyi painting should be described as a black-and-white art and an art with the addition and subtraction of black and white. In a limited picture increased black implies decreased white and vice versa addition in white implies subtraction in black. If in oil paintings, it is easy to do such addition and

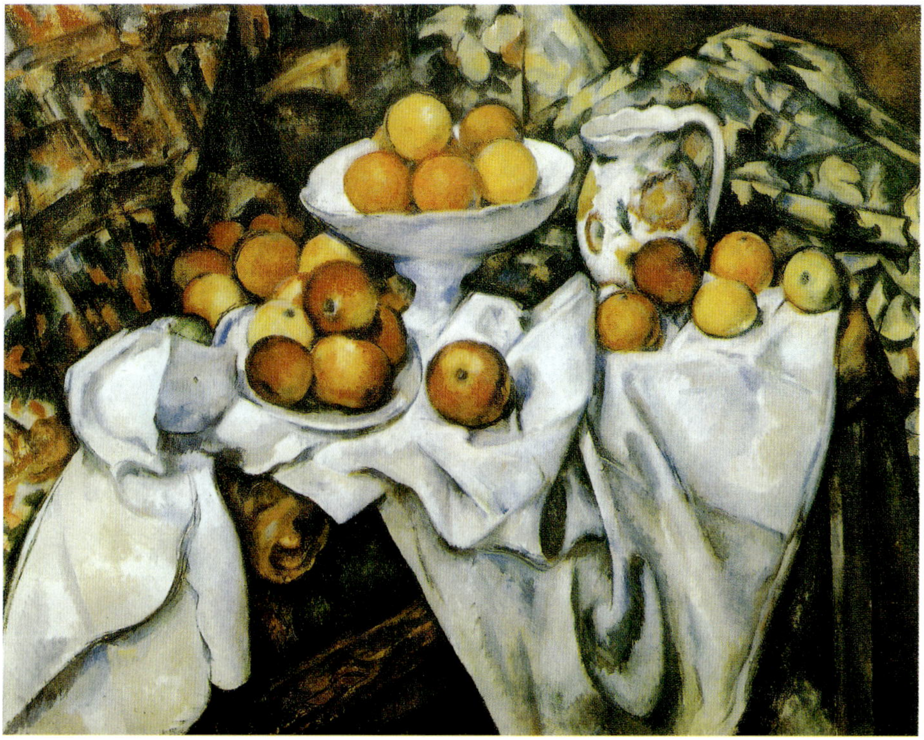

Still Life with Apples and Oranges: 1895-1900, oil on canvas 93 x 72cm, Paul Cezanne of France, Preserved in the Gallery of Impressionists in Paris

The compotier grows out of the beautiful white cloth, and the decorated jug seems to be a fusion of that cloth with the apples and oranges and the ornamented drape behind it. The effect is dense, even crowded, like his landscapes with woods and rocks, and is enormously rich in unexpected shapes and chords of color, almost to the point of engorgement.

subtraction; correct colours can cover incorrect ones to modify errors. This is not true for Chinese painting. Once the ink drops on the paper, black must be increasing and the addition cannot be reversed. A drop of black ink cannot be changed, deleted or covered by white. So it is difficult to do any additions in Chinese painting. As white as a colour is hardly ever used in water and ink painting, the white seen in a picture is almost always the blank space left on the white paper and the white decreases while the black increases. One touch of a brush will do both addition and subtraction with the attention on both black and white.

The method of leaving white shows the Chinese style of intelligence. First, the material is used to its utmost. Since there is blank space on white paper using white as a colour is useless. Applying a white colour on white paper shows disrespect to the raw material paper and is a waste of the colour. Second, when painting with a high degree of skill, painters can leave silk-like white spaces between the ink when increasing the black. Don't you think it is monotone and stiff if black and white are displayed on paper with clearly-divided borders? Crossed white and black can created a changeable picture. It is easy to realize crossed white and black with expected effects in European painting by overlapping the two colours but it is difficult in Chinese painting to apply one colour and arrange another colour at the same time. This is the thinking and actual way of Chinese people.

The technical addition and subtraction in Chinese painting cannot be grasped in a very short time. After the accumulation of time and experience and repeated experiments and careful study on the three tools of brush pen, ink and paper, such technique can be performed as an instinct and used with facility.

In the aspect of spirits, it should be by addition that gives painting that aesthetic feeling and meaning but Chinese aesthetic judgment is often represented by subtraction. In ancient times Chinese people adored conciseness. Confucius's *Lun Yu (the Analects of Confucius)* which was praised highly by later generations has only about 10,000 characters and the *Dao De Jing* of Laozi has only about 5,000 characters. Until the Song Dynasty (960-1279 AD) poems were more developed than prose passages in Chinese literature. The appearance of such phenomena was a result of restriction in technical conditions. When Laozi wrote *Dao De Jing* and Confucius wrote *Lun Yu* the Chinese people were writing on bamboo slips, so people would express their most concise thoughts by the most concise words to decrease the size of the bamboo slips. The Song Dynasty saw the arrival of light paper and moveable type printing but the books were made inefficiently and at a high cost, so people still liked the concise, beautiful and rhymed poems. Besides technical reasons, another important reason for Chinese people to adore conciseness is a rebellion in their subconscious. There were too many complex etiquettes in ancient times in China and although people dared not to breach or rebel against them they had a subconscious spiritual pressure and tiredness, so they needed concise cultural forms to release their spirits and hearts under this pressure and tiredness - they had a strong sense of identification with a concise form of art. In the poem *Village Travel* by Wang Yucheng from the Song Dynasty (960-1279 AD), 14 Chinese characters vividly depicted the scene of hills that are immersed in the light of the setting sun "Numerous voiced gullies contain the evening sound, countless silent peaks stand under the setting sun"); and in the poem of *Spring Moonlight on the Flowers by the River* by Zhang Ruoxu from the Tang Dynasty (618-907 AD), only 28 characters clearly expressed the poet's thoughts and his sigh with regret on life, nature and time "Who on the riverside first saw the rising moon? When did the moon above shine first upon the soul? After generations people will still come and go, while the river scene stays the same year after year"). It is this way of setting off by contrast in Chinese art and abundant mental thoughts are represented by concise forms. So also does this apply to Chinese painting. Pictures are usually the most concise images after simplification by painters in their hearts. They use general images, concise painting styles and simple colours to serve as a foil for their supreme minds. Looking at, the mountains painted by Ni Yunlin, you will feel a pretty cleanliness and brightness, the bamboo painted by Zheng Banqiao, you will taste his pride in his heart and watching the birds with white in their eyes painted by the Eight Great Hermits, you can acknowledge their aloofness and pride.

So, Chinese painting is an art combining contradictory addition and subtraction from technique to spiritual aspects.

ABSTRACTION, GENERALIZATION AND REPRESENTATION

Abstraction, generalization and representation are the painting skills often used in Chinese and western paintings. The difference between the two paintings is generalization is used less in western painting while generalization and representation have grown almost at the same time in Chinese painting.

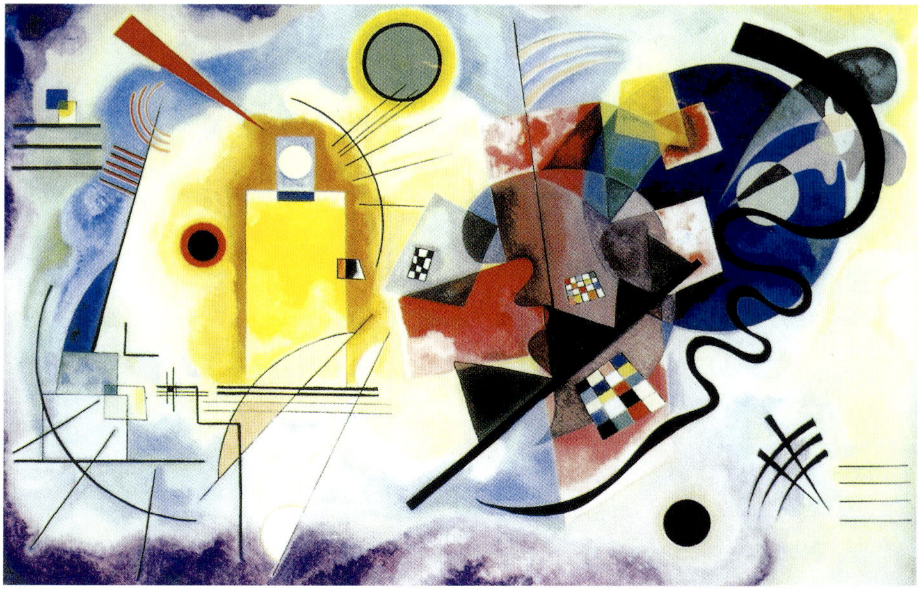

Yellow-Red-Blue: By Wassily Kandinsky of Russia, 1925, oil on canvas 127 x 200cm, Preserved in the Centre Pompidou, Paris.

In this painting, colors and lines have more expressive force of art. Although lines and colors are found in the geometrical forms, there is no careful handling. It is a freewheeling, improvisational, unintentional and free applying.

Representation and abstraction are directly perceived in western painting and it is easy to understand them. Most European paintings before the 19th century were representative and all the scenes and figures had similar models in real life. In the 20th century there appeared Abstractionism represented by a Russian Wassily Kandinsky who wanted to completely break away from real life art and who opposed the visualization of being true to life and the educational role of traditional paintings. He abandoned the former representative shapes and the method of painting. Since then there has appeared a "pure spiritual world" represented by symbols without concrete images or meanings. Abstraction was derived from its

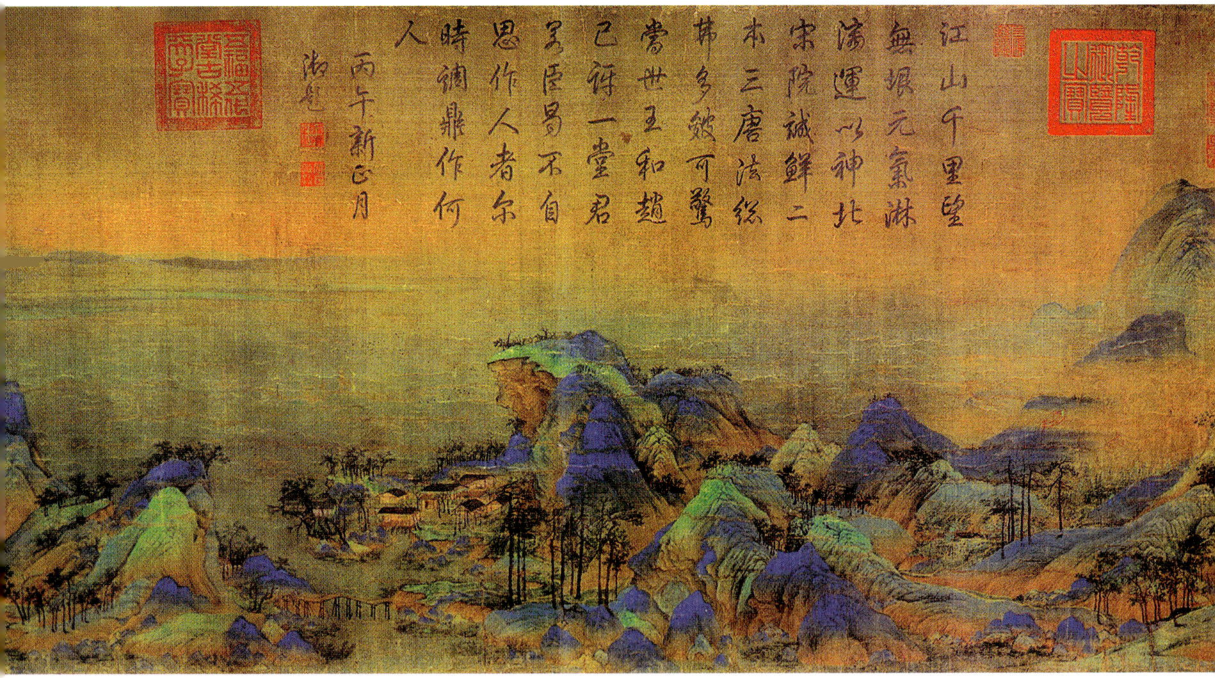

Qian Li Jian Shan Tu Juan (Scroll of Rivers and Mountains) (Part): By Wang Ximeng in the Northern Song Dynasty, Ink and color on silk 51.5 x 1191.5cm, Preserved in the Palace Museum in Beijing.

The painting depicts the mountains and rivers dotted with falls, springs, forest, villages, cottages, boats, bridges, and pavilions with the viridescence.

opposite, representation, in western painting.

The factors of generalization are mainly represented in western landscape paintings. Although painting definite trees and mountains, the western landscape paintings attach importance to the whole space sense and the sense of light and shadow and colours in the whole environment created by sunshine instead of just trees and mountains. The beauty created by light and shadow and colours in nature enchanted painters - the position of the sun is changing all the time, changes in sunlight result in continuous changes in colours in the natural environment and the whole atmosphere is also changing. Painters always want to record the most striking moments. Before super realistic painting, it is hard to see definite painting by tracing a leaf and what we see is only the general shape and the colours under the light and shadow of a tree. So, in western landscape paintings importance is not attached to a precise stone or a tree, but to generalizing the whole environment with its colours and atmosphere.

In Chinese painting generalization and representation have grown up at the same time. Landscape painting is an important branch in both Chinese and western painting but with enormous differences. In Chinese landscape painting an atmosphere is created in the course of painting realistically but it is different essen tially from the atmosphere created in European landscape paintings.

Chinese landscape painting is usually regarded as "mountains-and-rivers painting". The whole environment is also represented in Chinese landscape paintings but the importance is attached to each mountain and each stone. At the same time each mountain and stone is painted in a generalized way. *Model Paintings of a Mustard Seed Garden* is a series of books on painting techniques produced during the Qing Dynasty (1644 -1911 AD) and was worked out on the basis of many

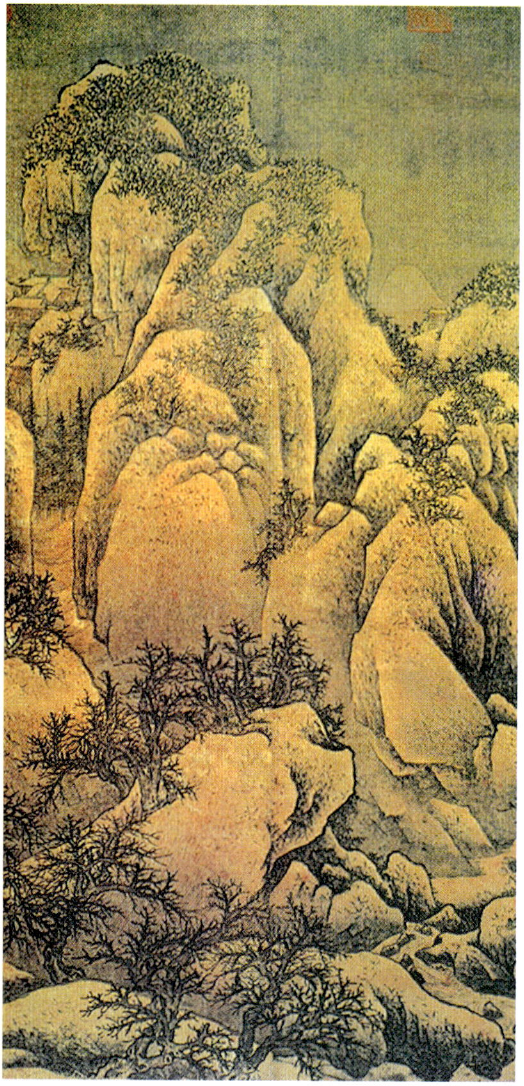

Xue Shan Xiao Si Tu Zhou (Scroll of Snow-capped Mountain and Desolate Temple): By Fan Kuan in the Northern Song Dynasty, Ink and color on silk 182.4 x 108.2cm, Preserved in the National Palace Museum in Taipei.

The peaks erect tall and upright. On the mountainside a desolate temple is seen gleamingly. The travellers walk in the mountains and by inns. Dense forest and strange stones can be found on the side and foot of the mountain.

paintings by former artists. According to the book, the traditional Chinese landscape paintings followed a pattern in aspects of the whole arrangement and the individual treatment on details similar to a symphony concert.

In western painting the remoteness and closeness in space is represented by the focus perspective while in Chinese landscape painting they are represented by false remote things and true close things. For example, in a landscape painting, even if a close tree is not the major object in the picture, you can see the trunk represented by simple vertical strokes but the remote trees have no trunk and they are only represented by several roughly painted strokes. Even with being rough, the trees are still vivid and will not be mistaken as anything else.

In Chinese painting almost all of the themes have a general set of ways which were summed up by generations of Chinese painters after more than a thousand years of observation and experience. They used formalized methods and generalized painting methods to show a true and vivid nature to people. For example, according to the differences between up-growing and down-growing branches, the deer-horn method and crab-claw method were summarized to paint them respectively. And according to different forms of needle-like leaves and broad leaves, more than 40 methods were summarized to represent them clearly, such as the "个 shaped point" and the "介 shaped point" in representing bamboo leaves which are proper in both Chinese words'shapes and painting styles.

In Chinese painting emphasis is placed on realm. There are two realms in Chinese painting. The first realm is "being similar in shape", i.e. the shape of the image is similar to the object. Generally speaking, the above-mentioned realm serves "being similar in shape" and focuses on appearance. In the other realm the appearance painting may be not realistic and exaggerated but the bearing of the objects is represented clearly. This realm is called "being similar in spirit". In terms of layers, "being similar in shape" should be the primary layer and is the standard requirement for beginner and inferior painters; "being similar in spirit" is a secondary layer higher than the former one and is the standard requirement for all top painters. The supreme realm in Chinese painting is "being similar to both shape and spirit" - the appearance and inside bearing are similar to the model, which is also the realm that all painters in China seek for.

Painting is at first visual and apparent. Why do Chinese people view realistically apparent shapes as the primary realm because Chinese people do not pay much attention to apparent things and think that the appearance of all things is only limited. For example, according to Chinese thought, no matter how tall, short, fat, lean, beautiful or ugly a man looks, it is not important, as he is only the body of a soul and thought and life is only a hundred years at most; but a lofty soul and a typical thought can exist and be passed down for tens of thousands of years. If a handsome man has a weak soul and a useless mind, he is only a common and valueless man. If an ugly man has a kind heart and a profound mind, he is a valuable and respectable man. So, it is easy to understand why Chinese people pay attention to minds instead of people: after all, most Chinese people are common, while exquisite matters condense numerous elements of human beings, such as intelligence, technique and economy and are portrayers of the comprehensive abilities of man at the time when they were created.

In the comparison of apparent shapes of matters, Chinese people pay more attention to the hidden internal spirit. Chinese people like to study the internal influence of matters: what factors result in differences between shapes of objects? What factors make the same things possess different qualities? These questions hover in Chinese people's minds and they hope to find such a mysterious control force. They find that the mysterious control force is invisible and intangible. The more mysterious objects appeared, the more they wanted to understand and seize this intangible thing. What they really hope is to represent the intangible dominator through a tangible form so as to grasp and comply with this dominator that was called "God" by Chinese people. But this "God" is much different from the "God" in west. The former one involves bearing, temperament and soul. So in the course of painting Chinese painters pay more attention to representation of the spirit. As long as the spirit of a thing can be represented completely, it is allowable to change the appearance a little. Essentially speaking, "being similar in shape" also serves as a way to realize "being similar in both shape and spirit".

So Chinese painting combines generalization and representation. The generalization in Chinese painting includes both the external generalization of techniques and the internal abstraction and generalization of the spirit.

PARTS AND THE WHOLE

Both Chinese and western paintings attach importance to the allocation of parts and the whole: excessive emphasis on some part will result in an imbalance of the whole, so painters pay special attention to the control of the whole. The whole picture is composed of all parts, so the treatment of each part cannot be careless. The allocation of parts and the whole is an important link for painters.

In western painting for both sketching and colouring, painters at first roughly confirm the whole structure, the position of each part and then do an in depth treatment. It takes time to go from light to strong strokes and the course is accomplished gradually.

It is different for traditional Chinese painting because it rarely has drafts. After painting on the paper the picture is finalized without any space for modification. So, all painters begin to paint after having a well thought out model in their minds eye. Some time ago a young man wanted to study painting bamboo after the style of Wen Tong and turned to a good friend of Wen Tong, Chao Buzhi, for a recommendation. Chao Buzhi often had drinks with Wen Tong and enjoyed looking at bamboo, so he knew how Wen Tong could paint bamboo so well. Wen Tong loved bamboo very much and planted various bamboos in the front and back of his house. Throughout the year, no matter whether it was sunny, rainy or windy, he would walk in the bamboo forest every day, observe the growth of the bamboos and think over the height and thickness of the bamboo branches and the shape and colour of the bamboo leaves. When he would get a new feeling, he would go back to his study, spread the paper, prepare the ink and paint the image of the bamboo in his mind onto the paper. As time went by, the different images of bamboo in different seasons, weather and time were impressed deeply in his mind. As long as he was standing in front of the paper and raising a brush pen with fixed attention, he would have all the various shapes of the bamboo before his eyes. Just as Wen Tong said, "Before painting bamboo, one must have a well thought out image of the bamboo in his mind." Chao Buzhi wrote a poem to the above-mentioned young man and two sentences of it are: "If you have well thought out images of bamboo in your mind then you can paint it well." As a result the phrase "being confident (with bamboo in mind)". became a classical idiom after being passed down to later generations. On the one hand it refers to the fact that painters begin to paint after thinking through the pictures and on the other hand it refers to the fact that people should take action after planning their project well.

Then, with well thought out pictures in the mind does it matter where to start painting? Yes, it does. The order of painting in Chinese painting is comparatively strict.

In nature many things give enlightenment to Chinese people.

In nature a river has a mainstream connecting all relevant tributaries and lakes along the way and each tributary and lake in the water system is only a part and a small feature and cannot represent the whole picture and features of the river. If one is studying the mainstream, it is possible to cover the features of all the tributaries and lakes along the way - after learning well the mainstream, one will learn well the

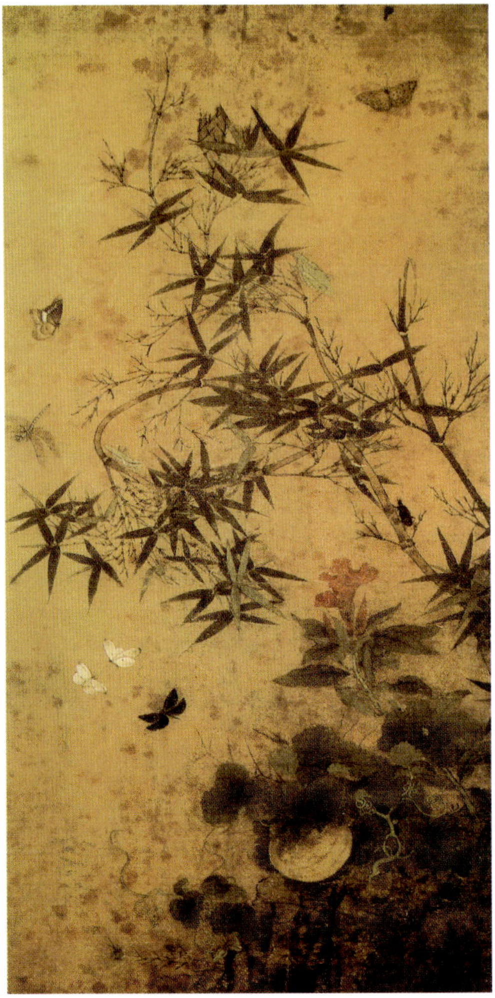

Zhu Chong Tu (Picture of Bamboo and Insects): By Zhao Chang, hanging scroll, Ink and colour on silk 99.4 x 54.2cm, Preserved in the Tokyo National Museum, Japan

This painting vividly represents the leaves of bamboo, distorted bamboo pole with light and dense colour, flowers, wild melons, flying butterflies and dragonflies, long-horned beetles, and long-horned grasshoppers. The painter imitated the technique of Xu Chongsi in drawing the melons, leaves and fruits, using dense colours.

ways and wherefores of all the tributaries and lakes.

Take a fallen leaf in autumn, the leaf blade erodes and only the veins are left which decide the basic form of the leaf.

When all the leaves have fallen off a tree only has its branches whose growth decides the shape of the tree.

...

These natural things make Chinese people attach importance to the veins that connect and decide the whole body.

From the point of view of the Chinese people, finding the veins and mainstream of an object or item thing means grasping the whole structure and shape of the thing. To this end Chinese people will make the effort to find the veins and the arteries of objects just as the veins of the body have been mapped out for acupuncture in traditional Chinese medicine.

Chinese people have fervent hearts

but they often express their emotions that are not easy to express directly, in other things. When Chinese painters regard some inanimate or immovable objects as persons, these objects will seem to derive the veins and expressions like a human. After these veins and expressions are grasped and transferred to paper, these inanimate or immovable things will become alive. For example, painting a mountain is compared to painting a man's face. You paint the nose at first then the cheekbone. Painters oppose painting from the parts to the whole and advocate painting the main trunk before the details. It means that the major horizontal and vertical veins of a mountain must be painted well first, with consideration to up, down, left and right and the relation between each part cannot be loose or close. This concept equals the composition of a picture from the beginning in western painting.

Chinese people paint an object as in the order of the veins from primary to secondary elements: paint the primary main shape first and then the composition and trend of the picture is fixed. Secondly, paint each part according to the requirements of the composition and the relation between black and white. When the picture is finished it must have reasonable composition and order between primary and secondary and vivid expressions.

The differences in treating the relationship between Chinese and western paintings can also be found in the treatment on the order of the parts and the whole.

Western people have a week hierarchy consciousness and a strong equality consciousness which are reflected in their paintings: all elements are treated equally without order and cared for comprehensively and the whole advances gradually. The relationship between the parts and the whole in a finished work is the same as the relationship between a major character and his foil.

In China there is a strict hierarchy between higher and lower authorities and

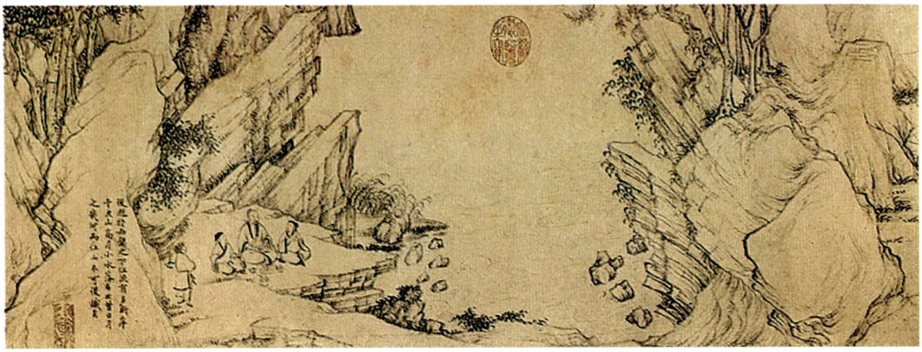

Scroll of Chibi: By Qiao Zhongchang in the Northern Song Dynasty, Ink on paper, Preserved in the Nelson-Atkins Museum of Art, the US.

The greatest value of this painting lies in fewer " water and ink " applied to the painting, a technique of drawing unseen in the landscape paintings before. This technique had been used a great deal until the Yuan Dynasty, while rarely in the works in the Song Dynasty. This shows Qiao Zhongchang's spirit of exploring in the drawing.

senior and junior people and the lower cannot surmount the higher and senior cannot offend the senior. This rule was stipulated to maintain stability and order and to form a good operation on the whole. With the extension to painting, there comes the difference between mainstream and tributary and the order of primary before secondary. In a finished work there is a dialectic relationship between the parts and the whole: they serve as foils for each other.

Breaking this order is not absolutely forbidden in Chinese painting but it is difficult to do so and the effects on the picture may not be good. For example, when painting a flourishing tree, according to traditional Chinese customs, you should paint the trunk first, the branches second and the leaves at the end - it is the order of growth. If you paint the leaves first, the branches second and trunk last, it will violate the natural growth rule of a tree. It will be a difficult task certainly. It is hard to paint growing relationships correctly and after painting the picture, due to incorrect relationships the picture will look bad. So, it is reasonable for Chinese painting to attach importance to the relationships between primary and secondary: the inability to modify in Chinese painting decides that there must be an order of painting between primary and secondary - the relationship of growth and between primary and secondary relationship in an object.

Again using painting a tree as an example, beginners of Chinese painting are required to grasp the "four-branch method" at first. It is based on the theory that the trunk and main branches are the most important and primary parts of a tree. After learning how to paint the trunk and the main branches, you can paint a complete tree when you add the leaves; without leaves, it is a withered tree in winter. If you can paint a tree well, you can paint a forest well.

There are several shapes for this "four-branch method": the trunk can have all the branches on the same side; the trunk is divided into two parts and the two main branches are divided into two branches respectively; the trunk grows horizontally and branches grow up; the branches are arranged along the trunk thinner and thinner from bottom to top; from bottom to top the branches alternate on each side, so that the tree will keep a balance. So, there are various shapes for the "four-branch method." After learning how to paint one tree, you can learn how to combine two, three or five trees. Why do people only study how to paint these combinations? Why aren't there combinations of four, six and more trees? Because according to symbolic logic, any natural number above four and five can be gotten by adding base units of the numbers of one, two and five. The three combinations have a special meaning. There are two kinds of combination for two trees: one big tree and one small tree, called "burden senior" and one small tree and one big tree, called "help junior". You may wonder, Aren't they both one big and one small tree? How to differentiate between "burden senior" and "help junior"? Both with a big and a small tree, the order of representation is not the same. Such order and naming shows the Chinese morality of respecting the senior and cherishing the junior.

As to the combination of three trees, the crowns of the three trees cannot be at the same height. Some are tall and some are short. The left and right one should modestly incline to each other and stand together naturally. This also shows the modest attitude of Chinese people.

As to the combination of five trees, they must be in two groups of three and two respectively and arranged alternately. This is changeable and not disorderly.

With the above-mentioned basic combinations, it is not difficult to paint a forest using different arrangements and combinations that reflect the Chinese people's concept on the organizational order of a whole composed of the parts.

Chapter VI: Dialectics between Motion and Rest

——Comparison of Representational Forms between Chinese and Western Paintings

Painting is a static art involving the dialectic relations between motion and rest. Both Chinese and western paintings involve motion and rest notwithstanding the differences between them. In term of the visual impression, western painting is dynamic while Chinese painting is static. Nevertheless, essentially speaking, Chinese painting is dynamic while western painting is static.

MOTION AND REST IN PAINTINGS

In term of visual impression western painting is dynamic. You can find motion everywhere in western paintings if you look carefully

In the picture on the ceiling of the Sistine Church, *The Creation of Adam* by Michelangelo, Adam, with strong, handsome muscles all over his body, was lying

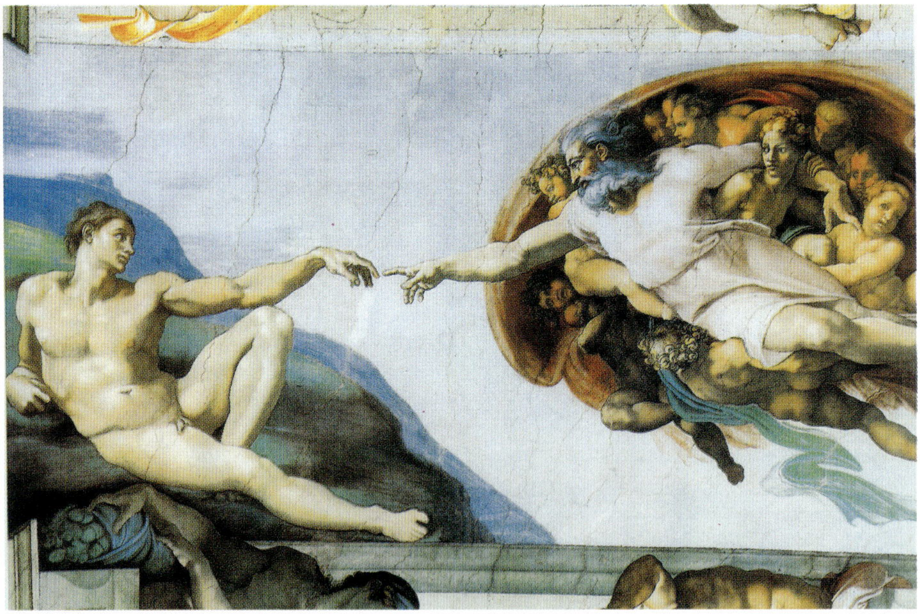

The Creation of Adam: 1510, a fresco on the ceiling of the Sistine Chapel, 280 x 570cm, by Michelangelo of Italy, Preserved in the Vatican City Museum.

It illustrates the Biblical story from the Book of Genesis in which God the Father breathes life into Adam, the first man. Michelangelo created the artistic world with its great talent as the God did.

on his side, spiritless, on a mountain slope and stretched out his left hand. As his life has not yet been injected, the expression in his eyes is empty and his arm is weak - he has to support himself using his knee. Jesus is flying in the sky with many angels clustering around. He is stretching out his right hand and is going to inject life into Adam. In this picture there is a strong sense of motion as the spiritless posture of Adam who is lying on his side and the flying Jesus create a visual instability.

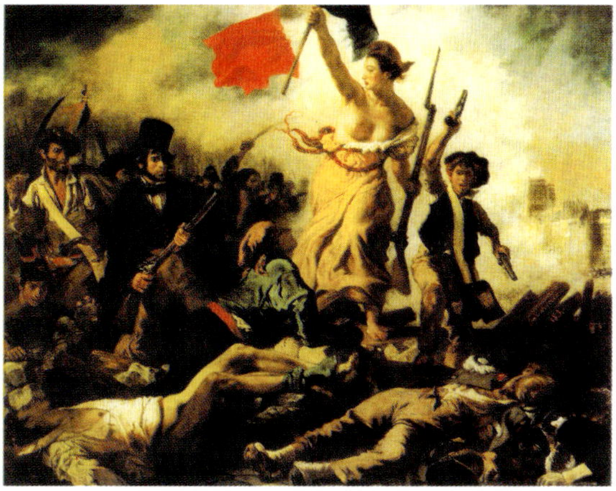

Liberty Leading the People: 1830, oil on canvas 260 x 325cm, by Eugene Delacroix of France, Preserved in the Louvre, Paris.
Probably Delacroix's best known painting, it is an unforgettable image of Parisians, having taken up arms, marching forward under the banner of the tricolour representing liberty and freedom. When displayed in Paris on May 1, 1831, it attracted strong response quickly.

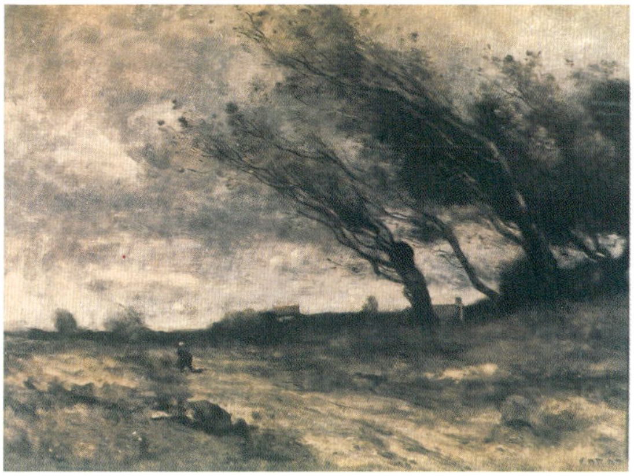

The Gust of Wind: 1865-1870, oil on canvas 46 × 58cm, by Camille Corot of France, preserved in Lans Museum of Fine Arts, France

In the painting, *Liberty Leading the People* by Eugene Delacroix, the posture of the Goddess of Liberty, walking ahead with her arms waving, forms a visual motion. At the moment when she turns her head back, all the people are answering her, forming a vocal motion.

In Raphael's mural *Galatea*, each human body represents a motion. In the *Gust of Wind* by Camille Corot there is a self-evident sense of the wind moving.

Western paintings with visual motion also contain the essence of stillness. Painting is a platform where painters record the scenes they have observed in paintings. It should be said that in western painting painters use dynamic pictures to record their static observation of a moment in time. The observation method adopted by western people is vertical focus as the sight of the observers is fixed and static and the representation on the picture is the freezing of the shapes for an instant. So, a static state can be found behind the dynamic forms in western paintings. Western paintings naturally contain rest in motion.

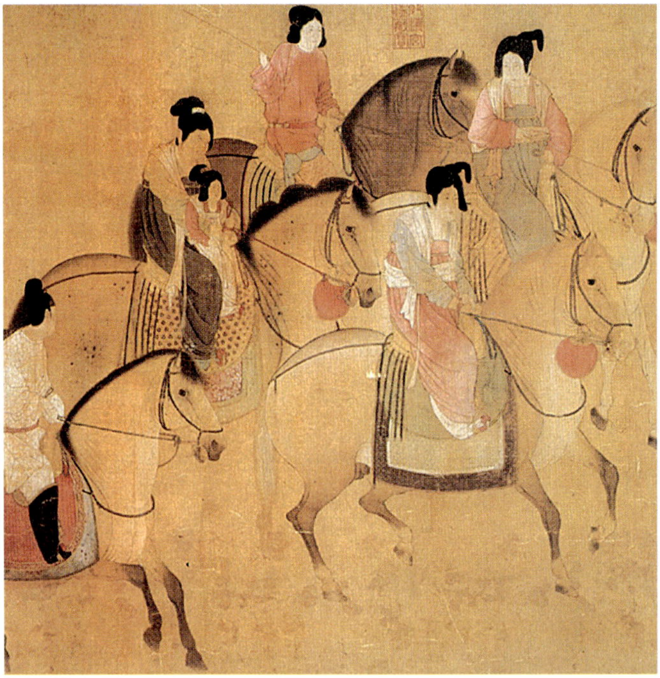

Guo Guo Fu Ren You Chun Tu (After Lady Guo's Spring Tour of the State) (Part): by Zhang Xuan (Copy in the Song Dynasty), Ink and color on silk, 52 x 148cm, Preserved in the Liaoning Provincial Museum.

This painting depicts the Lady Guo State, the elder sister of highest-ranking imperial concubine Yang, and her attendants riding on horses and taking a spring tour. The composition is harmonious, with the figures looking at each other with leisurely expressions and the horses stepping easily. It lively shows the warm spring.

In China, the shapes and lines in the paintings of the Warring States Period (475-221 BC) and the Han Dynasty

(206 BC - 220 AD) have very strong motion but in the literati paintings after the Tang Dynasty (618-907) the visual motion weakened a lot. *Guo Guo Fu Ren You Chun Tu (After Lady Guo's Spring Tour of the State)* is a painting with an outgoing theme. It should have been joyful and alive but it is not lively and makes people feel a lot of quietness. In another painting *Han Xizai Yeyan Tu (Night Revels of Han Xizai)* set in a home with a banquet and singing and dancing, it should be very joyful but the picture again reflects quietness. The landscape paintings in later ages focus mostly on mountains and stones and it is more difficult for people to feel "motion" in them - while the running water in the painted mountains further sets off the quietness of the mountains and the stones.

Chinese people adopted a horizontal, scattered observation method. The Chinese-style scattered observation method needs time to finish, so the scattered painting observation method both horizontal and vertical has advanced with time. When painters move their observation results onto paper, the contents of a particular time frame is frozen on the paper. The observation of a time frame is dynamic and the eyes of the observer are also dynamic. As to Chinese painting, a painter's dynamic observation of a time frame is recorded by a static picture, so the painting combines motion and rest.

MOTION AND REST IN REPRESENTATIONAL METHODS OF PAINTING

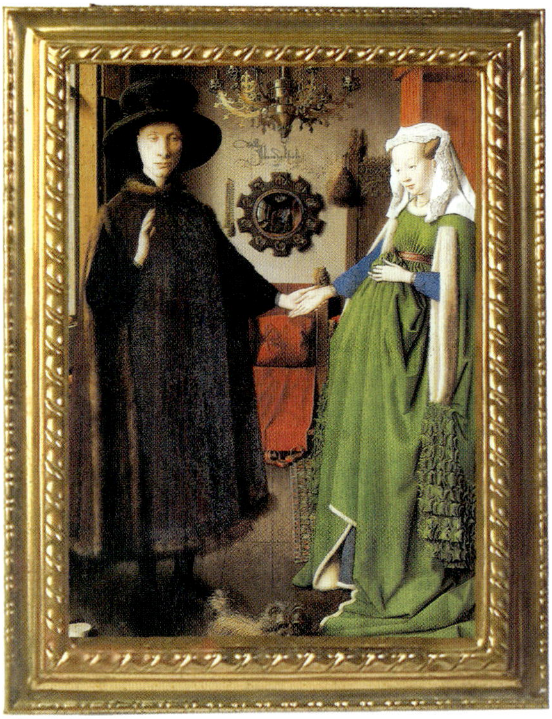

Western oil paintings are mostly framed

As to western painting, no matter whether it is an oil painting, a gouache, a watercolour or a sketch, most of them are square and surrounded by a picture frame. Inlaid in a square picture frame, western paintings are visually direct and give people a direct and concise impression.

This rapid and direct way in western painting seems to be related to the hunting life of an earlier time. In hunting only preciseness and rapidity can result in success and hunting cultivated the features of agility, preciseness and rapidity found in western people.

The creation and display style of western paintings decide that its manner of observation is nearly static. In terms of enjoying looking at paintings, the focus perspective in western paintings can at once attract the audiences' eyes to the main body of the pictures and the audiences' lines of sight are basically fixed without much range to move.

Like western oil paintings, Chinese paintings are also hung on the wall but most of them are not put in picture frames but hung directly on the wall like hangings. A few Chinese paintings are also shown in frames, such as xiaopian'er and fan face painting but painting on a scroll and hanging it on a wall is the original way of displaying a painting.

Chinese paintings possess a special form of appreciation and flavour in scrolls. When some one wants to show you a picture and brings along a scroll, you will start to have an expectation and guessing for an unknown thing. While the host expands the picture little by little, you will find that the scroll for Chinese paintings can

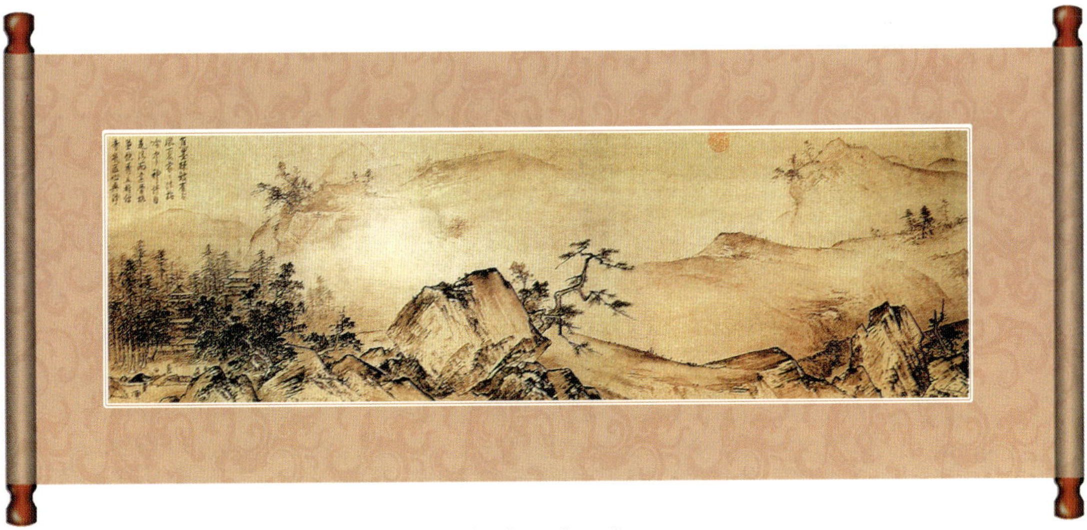

Chinese Landscape paintings are mostly in the form of scrolls.

represent Chinese thoughts and sentiments: when a scroll is opened you will first of all see a piece of long or short silk fabric (it is a silk fabric with designs on it. Today it is made by machine but in ancient times it was made by hand). As the picture is mounted flat and firm, the diagonal weaving of the silk fabric looks especially exquisite. After the prelude, you will see the blankness before motif - the edge on the picture paper. This is also a difference between Chinese and western paintings: except for some realistic paintings with strong colours, most of the traditional Chinese paintings will have some blank spaces left around the edges. Then the opening of the scroll slowly is accompanied by ups and downs in visual appreciation. This blank space makes the viewers eyes rest for a while and his or her heart which is full of expectation will calm down. Then the theme picture steps onto the stage ceremoniously. Due to the manner of opening the picture is expanded little by little. People will feel the ink techniques little by little and when the whole picture is shown, he or she can understand the theme, meaning and conception. This expanding course makes people's enjoyment and appreciation leisurely and unhurried. When you enjoy

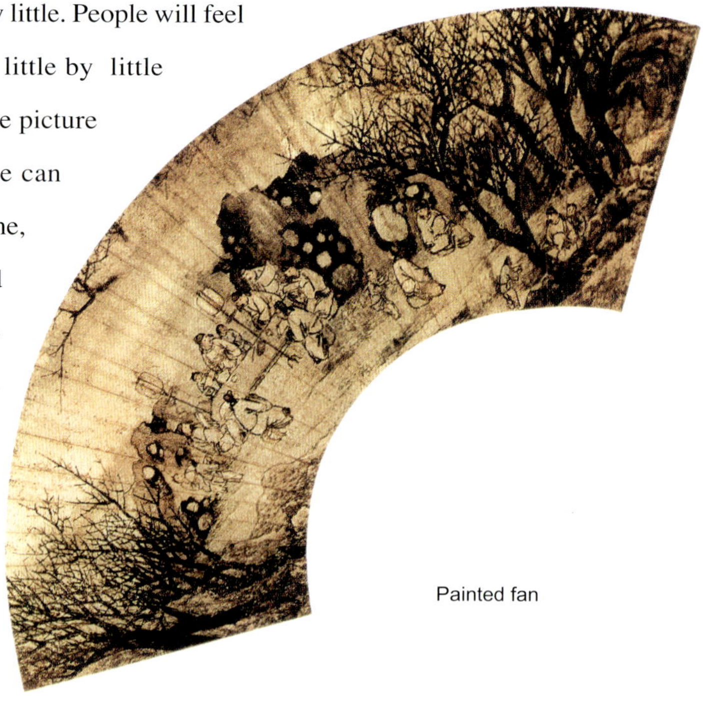

Painted fan

the picture alone or with others you will feel the comfort of the experience from the visual to the mind. After the main theme there is again a blank space and it ends with a piece of silk. It is an echo to start people's enjoyment, so that people's interests will not stop suddenly and the whole course of appreciation will remain satisfactory. The way to appreciate a scroll of painting seems like watching a drama. Before viewing the people get ready in spirit and the silk on each end seem like the on and off of the lights at the beginning and the end; the blank spaces left on both ends seem like the opening and closing of a stage curtain; and the theme of the picture seems like a drama and the preface, postscript and seal on the picture seem like an aside.

Of course, a scroll painting can also be put directly into a frame and hung on a wall like a western painting for people to appreciate visually. Then, the silk fabric with the paperhanging becomes the foil to the picture-paperhanging in China is a very professional art and technique, and a good paperhanging can show the ink layers vividly in their different shades.

The method of showing Chinese paintings is also the observation way: a Chinese painting is mounted on a scroll. If it is a horizontal scroll it will be opened slowly from right to left and if it is a vertical scroll it will be opened slowly from top to bottom, showing again the observation way which happens before painting the picture. The manner of viewing also represents a motion.

The appreciation of a fan face and a scroll is same. Most of the fans in ancient China had a bamboo or wooden framework pasted with paper and silk and could be folded to a very thin strip. When it is open it is in the shape of a semi-circle. In order to be pleasing to the eye, the fan face is decorated with painting and calligraphy. With the opening of a folded fan, the picture is exposed little by little. As a fan is a substantial matter and the shape of a fan face is fixed, there are more meanings and restrictions on fan face pictures for their decoration and design. It means that painters cannot paint at random on a fan face but must conform to custom the contents and forms of painting according to the sex, age, and identification of the user; and the contents, form and structure of the painting must be in harmony with the fan shape. Many famous painters painted fan faces in spirit and in the end some of them were not restricted by the substantial conditions and created paintings only according to fan face patterns and it became a specific painting form for pure appreciation, broken away from practicality.

Album painting is painting for pure appreciation. Its size is mostly equal to the size of the bookshelf containing it. Both paper and silk paintings are mounted and put into packets.

The creation and manner of showing of Chinese paintings is also influenced by the farming culture. The harvest is not decided by man-made elements in many cases and the same arduous labour will result in a good harvest during good weather and a bad harvest during bad weather. These elements will not change according to the joy or the annoyance of the people. So people learned to endure, not to lighten up with pleasure and lead a steady life. Then they had their leisure time and were interested in observing all things. The painting pattern followed and the manner of viewing that looked matter-of-fact but actually included the lifestyle of a thousand years. The expression of the scattered-points perspective makes each part of a picture include a story or sentiment, so the eyes of a viewer will move within a large range on the picture and form a dynamic feeling.

APPENDIX: A BRIEF INTRODUCTION ON CHINESE AND WESTERN PAINTING MATERIALS

On the basis of different materials, the common western paintings can be divided into the following major branches: tempera, oil, watercolour, gouache, propylene and sketch. The tools and materials include the pen (brush pen, oil painting stick, colour pencil, water-soluble colour pencil, charcoal, pencil, etc.), the interface (canvas and various kinds of paper or material) and dyes (mineral and chemical dyes).

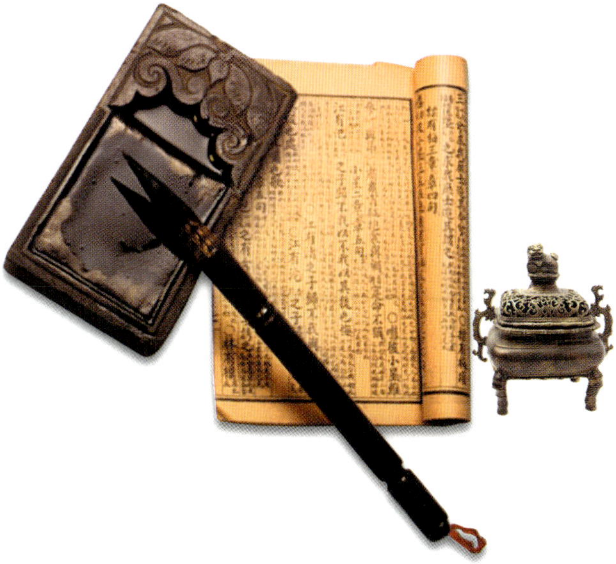

In traditional Chinese paintings, on the basis of materials, the major paintings are divided into silk and paper paintings. The materials include brush pen, ink, ink-stone, paper, silk and mineral dye. Among them the brush pen, ink, paper and ink-stone are called the "four treasures in study"

by Chinese people. They are not only the tools for painting but also independent treasures for people to collect.

It is necessary to stress that the tempera, oil, watercolour, gouache and propylene paintings in western painting also make use of a brush pen but it is completely different from a Chinese brush pen. The Chinese brush pen is made from animal hair fixed on a bamboo stick. Using varying force in touching the pen onto the paper, the pen point can show spots and lines with different sizes and thickness and the belly of the pen can be spread to paint a block and surface, so it can well satisfy the demand of Chinese painting for ease, verve, vividness and accomplishment without any letup. The brush pen handle used in western painting is also round but made of solid wood. In order to reduce the weight of the pen, it is mostly shaped fatter on the lower part and thinner at the end. It not only reduces the weight of the pen but also makes it easier to hold. The pen head is often compressed so that it can be used to paint a block and surface with the horizontal face and paint points and lines with the side face. In order to form a solid connection between the compressed pen tip and the handle, western people cleverly adapted a thin sheet of light metal to envelop it and the connection between the pen head and handle is extraordinarily solid.